ENDORSEMENTS

We are living in the last days. The devil is trying to kill, steal, and destroy. But God has raised up a bold prophetic voice that lives—and can teach you how to live—in all the promises of God. Becky Dvorak's teaching is your game changer!

SID ROTH
Host, *It's Supernatural!*

There are many books that have been written about the topic of death but I have not read one that covers the topic so thoroughly. Indeed we are all aware that this is one topic we will confront at least once in our life unless we are caught up to meet Jesus at the rapture! Becky Dvorak covers many of the crucial problems that happen when we stand by and let the enemy exercise his authority over our lives. As Christians we have the hope that the world needs and this book will answer many of the questions that need to be answered.

If you know someone who is dire need of hope and needs to know how to use the tools that Jesus gave us to conquer death and the enemy's assignments, this book is a must! Everyone needs to know how to walk in their authority as a believer and this book will help to show you how to do that.

Marilyn Hickey
Marilyn Hickey Ministries

There is much to be said about this great instruction manual, *Conquering the Spirit of Death*. The revelation and knowledge contained within its pages is priceless. It will cause you to abound in hope, and overflow with confidence in the promises of God. I am certain, once you've read it, the spirit of a conqueror will rise up "big" in you and the spirit of death will have to flee!

BARBARA BROWN
Senior Pastor
River of Life Worship Center, Odenton, MD

Becky writes "I read in His Word that I was more than a conqueror. What is a conqueror? A conqueror is a defeater, victor, winner, champion, a master of something. In this case, God's Word was teaching me that I was a master over satan—and so are you. When this gospel truth leaps off the page and gets deep into our hearts that we have the victory over him—he has to bow in defeat to us." Knowing Whose and who you are is always the key to VICTORY in CHRIST. In reality, we are victors before we even begin to experience the battle.

As in her other books, Becky under the inspiration of the Holy Spirit has undoubtedly simplified and exemplified the mystery of Christ's victory over satan, sin and death; for everyone who reads *Conquering the Spirit of Death* will learn how to enforce God's will for their life. I wholeheartedly endorse and recommend this book! You will be equipped and greatly empowered!

APOSTLE VICTOR and VICTORIA PHILLIPS
Faith Factor Ministries International
Niagara Falls, Ontario, Canada

I have seen great manifestations of the Kingdom of God moving with great power through the ministry of David and Becky Dvorak. I have seen broken people ministered to and the power of God completely restore them instantly, so that the crippled walk, the blind see, and the deaf hear.

In her new book, *Conquering the Spirit of Death*, Becky teaches us to know our adversary, and that he is a defeated foe. The Word of God is absolute power and authority. She tells us of His love for us, and that there is always hope in Jesus.

It has been an honor to know Becky, to watch as she loves people like Jesus loves, and see God move mightily through her ministry.

APOSTLE DON GRAY & PASTOR SHARI GRAY
Passion Ecclesia Church
Salisbury, North Carolina

Becky has done it again! Her latest work, *Conquering the Spirit of Death*, will inspire you to cross the threshold of impossibilities in practical ways! Her candid, sincere approach will impart the spirit of faith into your being and cause you to gaze into the face of the resurrected Christ. The real-life stories serve Heaven's verdict as a declaration of Life over death.

FAISAL MALICK
Lead Pastor, www.covenantoflife.org
Founder and President, www.plumblinenetwork.com

Since the middle of the 90s, we have followed Becky's work both in preaching the Word, being an author, and demonstrating her love and concern for the broken and lost. The care that she gives to the orphans is amazing; she truly is a blessing from God. These children and young adults have not only a great need for love and compassion but also a need for meeting with the power of God, through the atonement of Jesus Christ. What we have seen throughout Becky's life and service for God is a combination of being down-to-earth but still very dedicated to meeting with the individual person. Along with that, she has great faith and total certainty in the Holy Spirit, sharing His power for healing and deliverance.

In her book, Conquering *the Spirit of Death,* we get the right tools to work with and a deeper understanding of how this spirit actually is working. To read a book that includes such practical experience of spiritual warfare is a great privilege to all of us, both leaders and intercessors.

PASTOR LINDA BERGLING
Arken Church, Sweden

CONQUERING

THE SPIRIT

of DEATH

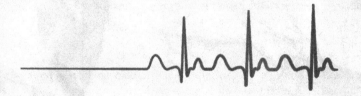

*Experiencing & Enforcing
the Resurrection Power of Jesus*

BECKY DVORAK

DESTINY IMAGE® PUBLISHERS, INC.

P.O. Box 310, Shippensburg, PA 17257-0310

"Promoting Inspired Lives."

This book and all other Destiny Image and Destiny Ismage Fiction books are available at Christian bookstores and distributors worldwide.

Cover design by Eileen Rockwell

Interior design by Terry Clifton

For more information on foreign distributors, call 717-532-3040.

Reach us on the Internet: www.destinyimage.com.

ISBN 13 TP: 978-0-7684-5058-3

ISBN 13 eBook: 978-0-7684-5059-0

ISBN 13 HC: 978-0-7684-5061-3

ISBN 13 LP: 978-0-7684-5060-6

For Worldwide Distribution, Printed in the U.S.A.

1 2 3 4 5 6 7 8 / 23 22 21 20 19

DEDICATION

I dedicate this work, *Conquering the Spirit of Death*, to those that are nearest and dearest to my heart; my husband, David; our children, Annie, Micah, Aaron, Ricardo, Jorge, Joaquin, Andres, and Marcos. And our added blessings; Adam, Rebecca, Deisy, Rose, and Vivi. And to all the joy created in our family; Addison, Jeremiah, Olivia, Joshua, Aubrey, Jonathan, Austin, Sarah, James, and Arwen. Together we walk in the glorious resurrection power of Jesus Christ and conquer the spirit of death.

ACKNOWLEDGMENTS

I would like to thank Destiny Image Publishers for their amazing job and professional touch to put this work, *Conquering the Spirit of Death*, together for you. Special thanks to Larry Sparks (publisher), Angela R. Shears (editor), Eileen Rockwell (cover designer), Terry Clifton (page designer), and John Martin (production manager). It's a privilege to work with you.

FOREWORD

The Bible says that the people perish for lack of knowledge. The Bible also declares that we (Christians) are seated with Christ far above all principalities, powers, authorities, and dominions. In this book, Becky provides personal experience, the Word of God, prayers, and pledges to equip you to defeat the spirit of death in your life and to enforce the victory of Jesus in the lives of other people.

Becky Dvorak spent twenty-five years in the trenches of service for Christ Jesus in an orphanage in Guatemala. God performed many miracles through Becky during that time, including the raising of the dead. Now the Lord is releasing Becky to equip the Body of Christ in the earth realm on a much greater scale. *Conquering the Spirit of Death* is part of that assignment. Do not perish prematurely concerning your destiny on earth. Conquer and destroy the spirit of death in your life and finish the race God has given you to run in the Name of Jesus.

PASTOR DWIGHT DUNBAR
Work of God Church
Mitchell, Indiana

CONTENTS

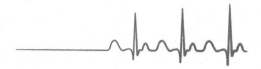

INTRODUCTION

We are living in the last days, when the attacks of the enemy are fiercer and more frequent than ever before. But even though times are turbulent, our God is still greater than satan and all of his demons, including the spirit of death, and all of their wicked works.

No matter the times we are living in, the facts of God remain the same. He created us to be more than conquerors, and to live life on this earth in His victory.

The pages of this work are designed to equip you in the faith, to shed spiritual knowledge about what you are fighting against, and how to overcome the spirit of death.

THE SPIRITUAL AND EMOTIONAL SIDE OF AN ATTACK FROM THE SPIRIT OF DEATH

Part One is dedicated to understanding the spiritual and emotional side of an attack of premature death. We will learn about the spirit of death, and some of its negative emotional partners. We will discuss why God is for us and satan is against us. And what part angels and demons play in all of this.

Chapter 1

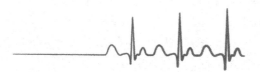

THE SPIRIT OF DEATH

WORD OF THE LORD

The Spirit of the Lord would say to you this day, "In this world you will have tribulation, you will pass through difficult times, but I say to you, 'I created you to win, to be victorious in every situation. I have equipped you with resurrection power, and that same Spirit that raised Me from the dead lives and resides within your very being. And I gave to you this same Spirit so that you could overcome the wiles of the enemy, that serpent of old. You be bold in who I created you to be—a conqueror, an overcomer, and victorious.'"

I can remember years ago, as a young believer in Jesus, I was unlearned about demons and the power of death, sickness, and disease that they carry. We never talked about such things, and it was certainly not taught from the pulpit I sat under as a child. Depending upon your affiliation of worship you were either expected to endure with the misconception that the evil attack was a blessing in disguise sent to you from God. Or you were expected to overcome with little to no training on how to do so—either stance often led to great tragedy, and it still does to this day.

And years later, while on the mission field I came under great physical attack. I knew it was not from God, but struggled to know how to be free from typhoid. The disease was in my body, and its attacks against my health were reoccurring. And each time it weakened my defenses against it, and it was worse than before.

This time it was a level 4, the worst it could be. My body was drained of all strength. I was fighting high fevers for days, and everything within me hurt so badly I just cried. The sickness took its toll on me, and I lost my desire to fight to live. And I asked the Lord to take me home.

But instead of allowing me to wallow in my pity, God rebuked me. He sternly said to me, *"Get up! Get out of bed! And get dressed!"* His words shook me down to the core of my being. They were what I needed to hear. They were an immediate wake-up call to what was happening to me. I was dying before my appointed time.

I immediately tried to get up, but my physical body was so weak I couldn't even lift my head off my pillow. I heard God's words again, *"Get up! Get out of bed! And get dressed!"* but this time they were not in the form of a rebuke, but an order. I tried again, but I didn't have the strength to sit up. Again, He repeated Himself, *"Get up! Get out of bed! And get dressed!"* At this point, I just slid out of bed and onto the floor. I slowly crawled to the dresser and got myself dressed. I then crawled to the door, managed to get it opened, and pulled myself up in the doorway. And as I walked down that long hallway, I regained my strength with every step. And from that moment on I was healed and never had another bout with typhoid again.

I had victory over typhoid, but something stronger was after me. I didn't know what was going on, but for the next several years, it was one serious attack of unrelated sicknesses after another.

In all honesty, I was fighting something I did not understand. It was something I could not see with my physical eyes, but I could see the results of it. And I thought these results (sicknesses) were the problem, but these were just the weapons of warfare being launched out against me. And the attacks were coming from all angles. The root issue was a spirit of death. This was what I was really fighting against.

There is an old adage that many of us have spoken time and time again, *"What you don't know can't hurt you."* Dear friend, this is very wrong—what you don't know can actually kill you. And this is certainly true with what we are confronting in this work. I am thankful I knew enough to go to God and find out what was happening to me.

While these physical attacks were going on, I was in the Word night and day. This was the only thing I knew to do—seek God and His Word with everything within me. This is what delivered and healed me. It not only set me free, but equipped me to train you. The benefits gained from a life spent in the Word of God are beyond measure.

I read in His Word that I was more than a conqueror. What is a conqueror? A conqueror is a defeater, victor, winner, champion, a master of something. In this case, God's Word was teaching me that I was a master over satan—and so are you. When this gospel truth leaps off the page and gets deep into our hearts that we have the victory over him—he has to bow in defeat to us.

> *What then shall we say to these things? If God is for us, who can be against us? Who shall bring a charge against God's elect? It is God who justifies. Who shall separate us from the love of Christ? Shall tribulation, or distress, or persecution, or famine, or nakedness, or peril, or sword? Yet in all these things we are more than conquerors through Him who loved us* (Romans 8:31,33,35,37).

With the revelatory workings of hindsight, I understand why the attacks were so severe and unrelenting against me. If the enemy could stop me before I realized the depth of the calling on my life, he would win a great battle, and there would be a lot of casualties in my defeat against death. We all have an arena of influence, ordained by God, and my arena is to help you heal. It's important that we seek God for the revelation of the root and the reason for the enemy's attack against us.

Then one night while praying in the Spirit—in tongues—I felt led to lay my hand upon myself and renounce a spirit of death that was attacking my body. As I spoke these words aloud, *"In the name of Jesus I renounce a spirit of death. I command it out of my body!"* I almost vomited when I felt something literally come up and out of me with a force. And I was free from the attacks of the enemy in this area.

What do I mean when I say, "I renounce a spirit of death"? The word "renounce" means to cast off or reject, as a connection or possession; to forsake; as, to renounce the world and all its cares.[1] So, when I renounce this spirit of death, I cast it off me and reject its connection with me.

It is very evident to me that today many are in need of this teaching as well. This week alone, the prayer requests from my readers are filled with distress calls for deliverance and healing from the spirit of death that is rising against them in many forms.

God's people are crying out for deliverance from a spirit of suicide, for encouragement and a reason not to abort their children, for divine intervention and protection from near deadly attacks from abusive family members and demon-possessed strangers.

Many others are seeking help to heal from the last stages of breast cancer, prostate cancer, kidney failure, and rare and incurable diseases.

The news is filled with disasters that are sweeping the lives of hundreds and thousands off this earth and into an eternity in hell with no hope of escape. And not so popular in the news, whether it be Christian or secular sources, is the onslaught of persecution of our Christian brothers and sisters around the world who are being martyred for their faith in our Lord Jesus Christ.

As followers of Jesus, how do we respond? How do we go beyond just mere survival in these last days, and step into the promise that we are more than conquerors, and actually defeat and conquer the spirit of death?

God wants us to know how to conquer this spirit of death. He wants us to have His full revelation concerning our victory in Christ. His Word so beautifully tells us in Second Corinthians 2:14, *"Now thanks be to God who always leads us in triumph in Christ, and through us diffuses the fragrance of His knowledge in every place."*

Let's pray.

> *Dearest Holy Spirit,*
>
> *You are our Teacher, and we ask You to diffuse the fragrance of Your knowledge in every place so that we might triumph in Christ. Glory be to God in the manifestation of this revelation in our lives that we are more than conquerors, including victory over the spirit of death. In the mighty name of Jesus, we pray, amen.*

THERE IS ALWAYS HOPE WITH JESUS

The number-one revelation we need to accept is that with Jesus, there is always hope. Hope for a new beginning, hope for a creative miracle, hope for deliverance, hope for financial provision, hope for forgiveness, hope for healing, hope for salvation, hope for restoration, hope for resurrection, and hope for a total transformation in any situation we face.

Why? Because our Savior knows no lack, has no limitations. He operates by faith on our behalf in the power of His redemptive blood that He so graciously shed for us. He is up in Heaven interceding on our behalf, cheering for us to overcome all tribulation on this earth, including the spirit of death itself.

With this revelation that there is always hope with Jesus, we are ready to take the first step in this battle.

KNOW YOUR ENEMY

The first step in any battle is to know who your enemy is, otherwise you will engage in combat with your fellow soldiers and your allies—those who are sent to help. The word "ally" comes from the Latin word *alligare*, meaning "to bind to," like nations who are allies in wartime, they will act together, and protect one another.[2] God and His heavenly hosts of angels are your allies, and the believing believers are your fellow soldiers in this fight.

And yes, you are caught up in a battle, a very personal one. And unless you know who your real enemy is, you can't win the fight. God knows full well that His enemy is satan and the harm he commits against us. This is one reason why He sent His Son Jesus, *"that He might destroy the works of the devil"* (1 John 3:8).

But many people don't believe Him nowadays. In fact, many who once believed God's Word now claim there is no hell, there is no devil, and everything that happens, whether good or bad, comes from God. First Timothy 4:1 tells us, *"Now the Spirit expressly says that in latter times some will depart from the faith, giving heed to deceiving spirits and doctrines of demons."*

So in the middle of this spiritual confusion, they lose the battle because they are unsure about who their real enemy is, and what they actually fight against. And they battle this confusion within themselves as they believe all things, both good and evil are from God, and why would God do this to them. It ends up to be a losing battle that they just can't win.

And this is how it is with the workings of confusion and double-mindedness—you can't win. You become unstable in all your ways. (See James 1:8.) You can't stand firmly against an enemy you don't believe in.

And to reiterate, you must know who your real enemy is in order to conquer and win.

This war is not against one another. It's not against your doctor, your spouse, your children, your pastor, or your friend, but against things we cannot see with the natural eye. The Bible tells us in Ephesians 6:12, *"For we do not wrestle against flesh and blood, but against principalities, against powers, against the rulers of the darkness of this age, against spiritual hosts of wickedness in the heavenly places."*

And make no mistake we're in the midst of a spiritual war against spiritual hosts of wickedness in heavenly places. But we are not alone in this fight, God and His heavenly host are with us, fighting satan and his demonic force on our behalf. Romans 16:20 assures us with this promise of victory, *"The God of peace will soon crush Satan under your feet. The grace of our Lord Jesus be with you."* This is an unseen fight between God and His goodness and satan and all of his evil. And we're encamped between two supernatural forces, God and His angels, and the devil and his demons. This is a genuine combat between life and death, both eternal and natural. It's best that you have a clear understanding just who your fellow soldiers and allies are in Christ, and bind yourself with them—not with the enemy and his legions of demons.

WHAT IS THE SPIRIT OF DEATH?

The spirit of death is a demon, a very powerful one bent upon our destruction to provoke premature death in our physical bodies. It works with a team of demons, such as a spirit of fear, a spirit of infirmity, and others too. We will discuss these throughout this work.

This death that I am referring to here is not to be confused with what's discussed in Scripture about an appointed time to die. The following verses tell us God's plan for the death of His children:

To everything there is a season, a time for every purpose under heaven: A time to be born, and a time to die... (Ecclesiastes 3:1-2).

You shall come to the grave at a full age, as a sheaf of grain ripens in its season (Job 5:26).

...You take away their breath, they die and return to their dust (Psalm 104:29).

God's plan for us is that we live to a ripe old age; and when we fulfill the time He has allotted for us, He takes our breath away. There is no pain and great suffering. We simply pass from this earth and into our eternal destination. And this answers a common question asked by many, including a faithful reader and friend, Martha, "Under what circumstance is the end?"

Therefore, the spirit of death that is being referred to throughout this work is premature death, when the life of someone is being stolen before their appointed time and is usually very tragic in nature, and includes incidents of fatal accidents and suffering through sickness and disease, suicide and murder, including abortion. An example of the work of the spirit of death is a young woman, a faithful wife and mother, whose body is being attacked by a deadly cancer, beginning with metastatic breast cancer that spreads to her lungs and to her brain. God is not the author of this type of death. Jesus paid a high price with His blood for the healing and deliverance of this precious woman. This is premature death and the spirit of death is fighting hard to take this woman out before her appointed time, before she can fulfill her destiny. This is tragic and demonic in every way.

First Peter 5:8 from the Amplified Version of the Bible warns us like this: "*Be sober [well balanced and self-disciplined], be alert and cautious at all times. That enemy of yours, the devil, prowls around like a roaring lion [fiercely hungry], seeking someone to devour.*"

THE TACTICS OF THE SPIRIT OF DEATH

The tactics of the spirit of death go hand in hand with satan's strategies against us found in John 10:10, *"The thief does not come except to steal, and to kill, and to destroy...."* What does the spirit of death steal from us? The spirit of death steals the fulfillment of hopes and dreams, a full lifetime of togetherness for couples, families, and friends. It robs parents from their children and children from their parents—the list of its thefts is endless.

What does the spirit of death kill? Despite the obvious, the killing of the physical body, the spirit of death kills much more. This murderous spirit kills off the God-given destiny of individuals and the influence they are meant to have on the lives of the people in their arena of influence.

What does the spirit of death destroy? The spirit of death destroys the witness of the individual of a loving God who truly loves and cares for all people, and is willing and able to heal all sickness and disease.

This is just a list of a few areas that the spirit of death steals, kills, and destroys. You are well aware of the tactics of evil that are ravaging in your own life.

A List of the Spirit of Death's Deadly Operations
The deadly operations against us, to name just a few, include weapons of mass destruction such as sickness, rare and incurable diseases, lying spirits that induce thoughts of suicide and murder, including abortion, and all types of terroristic attacks.

HOW DOES IT GAIN ACCESS?

The spirit of death is sly and cunning, and it works in the realm of spiritual darkness. It first enters into the mind and the emotions when we least expect it. Especially, when we lack time in the Word, our faith level dwindles, and our spiritual defenses are easy for the enemy to breach. Or when we fall ill, we tend to let our spiritual guard down, and the enemy takes advantage of this spiritual weakness. The spirit of death also has a vicious appetite for the vulnerable and unsuspecting people of this world. These are some common inroads where it gains access to do its evil.

Telltale Signs That a Spirit of Death Is Attacking You

The following is a list to help you discern whether or not you are being attacked by a spirit of death.

- You are diagnosed with a rare and/or incurable disease.
- There is an onslaught of sickness and disease reoccurring in your body.
- You are battling with discouraging thoughts to give up the fight and die.
- You are dealing with a barrage of accidents and strange events that can lead to death.
- You are struggling with suicidal thoughts.
- You are fighting with murderous and terroristic thoughts against others.
- You desire to abort your baby.
- You continuously engage in behaviors and activities that invite death, such as reckless driving, life-threatening sports, drug and alcohol abuse, and other negative habits that display a death wish.

A LITTLE GIRL'S ATTACK FROM A SPIRIT OF DEATH

On December 26, 2018, Victor wrote requesting prayer for his little girl: "Dear Becky, please pray for my 3-year-old daughter who has been suffering from epileptic seizure disorder for about 7 months now. I believe in the spiritual authority and God's grace for healing upon you and I am confident that my daughter will be completely healed when you pray for her. Thanks."

A spirit of death, along with an epileptic spirit attacked this little girl and tormented her with deadly seizures. And yes, demons do not play fair, they go after vulnerable prey such as this little girl who is unable to defend herself. But her parents recognized this as an attack of satan, and exercised their God-given authority over their daughter and activated their covenant rights with the Father through the redemptive blood of Jesus to free their daughter from these demonic works.

Cast a Spirit of Death Out

When it comes to a spirit of death or any demon for that matter, you have the spiritual right, along with the responsibility, to cast it out of the individual, whether it is you or another person. Either you cast it out, or you find someone else to cast it out for you, as in the real-life situation of Victor and his daughter. The following is what happened when the father of this child and I communicated about the needs of his daughter.

I responded with a prophetic prayer of faith for her deliverance and healing: "In the name of Jesus, I renounce this spirit of death, epilepsy, and seizures attacking your daughter. I release the healing power of Jesus to flow in and throughout her brain. I command all pathways that have been dug out in her brain for seizures to follow to be supernaturally erased for the glory of God, and no new pathways for seizures may be formed. I decree no more seizures because there is no more epilepsy for the glory of Jesus, amen and amen."

The Report of the Manifestation of Her Miracle

A week later, on January 2, 2019, Victor wrote to testify of his daughter's glorious healing: "Dear Becky, the Almighty God is indeed still in the business of doing the impossible and the miraculous. I can confirm to you that the seizures have all stopped; this is so breathtakingly miraculous. My family and I are completely dazed and awed at the power of God at work. It happened just like that. My daughter has regained her perfect state of health. The most astonishing fact is that she got completely healed before we crossed into the New Year. Now, we are confident that she can resume school with her peers after the holidays. Oh, Jesus Christ is indeed the same yesterday, today, and forever. We stand amazed at the power of the Almighty God. To Him be all the glory, honor, and adoration forever and ever."

IT'S YOUR TURN

Perhaps, you just can't seem to get free from death, sickness, and disease, as in my opening testimony, or in the situation of this little girl. Lay your hand on your body and renounce this spirit of death coming against you with the authority that comes from the active blood of Jesus Christ within you. Command it out of your physical body in the name of your Healer—Jehovah Rapha.

Say, "In Jesus' name, I renounce this spirit of death. I cast you out, leave this body at once!" And begin to pray in your heavenly language—tongues.

THE INTIMIDATION OF THE ENEMY

Is the enemy trying to intimidate you by telling you that you can't do this? When he tries to play his games of intimidation with me, I know he is afraid of what I am about to do. And I share this with you to give you a heads-up. When the enemy is taunting you with intimidation, you play his bluff, put a smile on your face and start to laugh, because you are about to win.

In the next chapter we discuss how negative emotions partner with the spirit of death against us.

Prayer

> *Dear Holy Spirit,*
>
> *I find myself in a battle with the spirit of death and my body is suffering from sickness and disease. I've known it's not from you, but I have not known how to be free from this. I desire Your wisdom in dealing with the spirit of death. I need to be wise in this area of life, so that I can protect my family and myself from its deadly attacks. Help me, Holy Spirit, to study Your Word concerning this so that I do not have to be ashamed because I was naive when it came to demons and the power of death, sickness, and disease that they carry. Show me how this demon works against me and those I love; train me in Your Kingdom ways to beat this attack and conquer the spirit of death, in the name of the Father, Son, and Holy Spirit, amen and amen.*

Pledge

I pledge to God and myself to study His Word to gain a deep understanding about the tactics of my enemy so that I can defeat and overcome the spirit of death, to walk in the victory of my Lord, and to fulfill my destiny in the mighty name of Jesus, amen.

Questions for Chapter 1—The Spirit of Death

1. What does the word "renounce" mean?

2. Why is it important in a battle to have a clear understanding of who your enemy is?

3. What is the Latin word for *ally*? And what does it mean?

4. What is the spirit of death?

5. The tactics of the spirit of death go hand in hand with who and what?

6. How does the spirit of death operate against us?

Personal Reflection

As I read through this first chapter, am I being attacked by a spirit of death? Am I struggling with any of the telltale signs discussed in this chapter? Am I willing to learn what I need to do to be free from this?

Group Discussion

Together as a group discuss the telltale signs that a spirit of death is attacking someone. Are any of these signs manifesting in your life? If so, pray for one another in faith and renounce the stronghold of this demon over you and your loved ones in the name of Jesus.

ENDNOTES

1. *KJV Dictionary*, s.v. "Renounce," https://av1611.com/kjbp/kjv-dictionary/renounce.html; accessed May 30, 2019.

2. Vocabulary.com, s.v. "Ally," https://www.vocabulary.com/dictionary/ally; accessed January 5, 2019.

Chapter 2

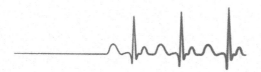

NEGATIVE EMOTIONS PARTNER WITH THE SPIRIT OF DEATH

WORD OF THE LORD

The Lord would say to you this day, "Listen and learn what My Spirit is teaching you this day. You have read in My Word that it is the little foxes that spoil the vine, so too it is the seemingly harmless emotions that partner with the spirit of death that open up the vile doors of the devil and all his wickedness against you. Listen and learn what My Spirit has to say to you this day."

You might be asking yourself, How did this happen? How is it that my body is racked with sickness and disease and even death? Or maybe you are unsure how to minister to a loved one facing this situation. You ask, How do I encourage and pray for this individual effectively? How do I shed light into the darkness of this person's present situation? How do I give hope to the one who feels hopeless? God's Word has the answers to these questions, and so much more.

First of all, sickness, disease, and hard times often open the doors to negative feelings. And even though things like discouragement, depression, and anxiety in the beginning may seem harmless enough, it's amazing how they along with other negative emotions quickly partner with the spirit of death and wreak utter havoc in our lives.

FEAR

One of these partners is fear. People fear many things such as bugs, spiders, bats, snakes, darkness, lack of provision, being alone, rejection, germs, sickness and disease, and this list goes on and on—but the thing most people fear more than the rest is death.

> *Inasmuch then as the children have partaken of flesh and blood, He Himself likewise shared in the same, that through death* **He might destroy him who had the power of death,** *that is, the devil, and* **release those who through fear of death were all their lifetime subject to bondage** (Hebrews 2:14-15).

The Bible warns us that *"the thing I greatly feared has come upon me, and what I dreaded has happened to me"* (Job 3:25). Fear is a serious matter, and usually can be controlled. But when we allow it to fester within us, it becomes dangerous, and even deadly, as it works against us with a spirit of death.

This fear of death is very real, and it is more than a negative emotion—it's spiritual, and it's demonic. Second Timothy 1:7 says, *"For God has not given us a spirit of fear, but of power and of love and of a sound mind."* I have found during my many years in the healing ministry that a spirit of fear travels with sickness and disease. It is often the forerunner of a spirit of premature death. It takes a decision on the part of people who are gravely ill to not give into this spirit, and force themselves into the arena of faith where power, love, and a sound mind exist.

And Jesus more than anyone else understands this battle. In the Garden of Gethsemane, He knew He was about to be slaughtered for all people and that the suffering would be so torturous that He battled fear and sweat great drops of blood. (See Luke 22:41-44.) He was tempted to give up, but He overpowered this fear by faith and prayer. And this is how we will too.

I receive many prayer requests daily from God's people needing prayer for healing. They have received a very serious medical report and the fear of death has taken over their mind and emotions. But before the prayer of faith can take effect, this spirit of fear has to be dealt with.

Fear paralyzes the spiritual tongue, and then it affects the rest of the body. Why? In Proverbs 18:21 it says that life and death are in the power of the tongue. Your tongue possesses a power.

What is this power? It is the power of the spoken word. Words have the power to create or to destroy. This is why fear, first and foremost, paralyzes the healing power of the tongue. If you receive the injection of its venomous poison into your spirit, you will begin to speak failure, destruction, and even death. And by the power of your own tongue, what you speak will come to pass.

I know a young man who became very ill and was in a lot of pain. It was soon discovered that he had a cancerous tumor on his pancreas. He shared with me what happened to him when the doctors came into his hospital room to give him the bad report. He said that as he heard the death report, he could not speak. It was as if he had swallowed poison. What did he really swallow? He swallowed fear—more precisely a spirit of fear. He accepted this death report and a spirit of death entered into his spirit and immediately began to meditate and speak death.

It took others to speak words of hope and healing into his life in order for his faith to be encouraged to the point that he accepted the words of faith and started to speak them for himself. And once he started to speak faith-filled words of healing, health, and life, his miracle manifested and the cancerous tumor disappeared, and it never came back.

It is of extreme importance that we protect ourselves from the spirit of death and refuse to accept its venomous poison—the spirit of fear.

Isaiah 41:10 (AMP) encourages us with these words: *"Do not fear [anything], for I am with you; do not be afraid, for I am your God. I will strengthen you, be assured I will help you; I will certainly take hold of you with My righteous right hand [a hand of justice, of power, of victory, of salvation]."*

Four Scriptural Measures to Overcome Fear

1. **Set your thoughts on godly matters, instead of earthly ones.** Paul, an apostle of Jesus Christ, by the will of God writes to us in Colossians 3:2, instructing us to *"Set your mind on things above, not on things on the earth."* Refuse to dwell on the negative reports and force your mind and emotions to focus on the promises of God. It may seem like false faith in the beginning, but you have to take this first initial step to transform fear into faith.

2. **Give your worries to God.** Peter, another apostle of Jesus Christ, in First Peter 5:7 encourages us with these words, *"Casting all your care upon Him, for He cares for you."* Ponder upon God's Word that He truly does love and care for you. And that He will faithfully see you through the situation.

3. **Pray in tongues and encourage yourself.** Again, the apostle Paul teaches us in First Corinthians 14:4 (NIV): *"Anyone who speaks in a tongue edifies themselves...."* When fear tries to overwhelm you, start to pray in tongues. Encourage yourself throughout the

day and night by praying in in your heavenly language—it works.

4. **Choose to think upon the positive promises of
   God.** Paul, also referred to as a bond-servant of Jesus
   Christ, writes to us in Philippians 4:8 (NIV): *"Finally,
   brothers and sisters, whatever is true, whatever is noble,
   whatever is right, whatever is pure, whatever is love-
   ly, whatever is admirable—if anything is excellent or
   praiseworthy—think about such things."* Choose what
   you think about. If it doesn't align itself to the message
   of this verse, toss it out of your mind.

A WORD OF THE LORD

And the Spirit of the Lord would say to you this day,

> *Why do you continue to live in fear? Do you not know that I
> am forever near? I will never leave you, nor forsake you. I have
> given My angels charge over you to protect you. I have sent My
> Son, Jesus, to break the bondage of fear. So why do you continue
> to bind yourself to its wickedness? My Holy Spirit is with you to
> lead you and guide you into all truth. The truth in My Word
> will set you free. Come under the safety of My wings, do not
> leave the perimeter of My presence. Carry My presence with you
> wherever you go. I love you with an everlasting love, and it's My
> perfect love that casts away all fear.*

Let's Pray

Call out to the Father right now and confess to Him your fears,

> *Father God, I am fearful that I will not ever feel well again, that
> my healing might not manifest. I feel insecure that I do not mea-
> sure up to You and to others. I am afraid of being alone. Father,*

forgive me for taking in and sheltering this spirit of fear. Right now, by faith I am giving it an eviction notice and it must leave the premises of my temple now! Help me, Holy Spirit, to remember that I do not need to fear, that I am as bold as a lion, and more than a conqueror, in Jesus' name I pray, amen.

Pledge

I pledge by the power of Holy Spirit within me that with God's help I will work on overcoming all fear in my life. I will not allow fear to inhabit my being. When it comes to such things as creepy-crawly creatures of nature, I promise to work on controlling my feelings, and to be rational about these matters. And as I learn to activate my authority in Christ over these natural matters, I train myself to overcome fear in more important matters in life. I will hold my peace in the face of the spirit of death. I will also activate victory over fear and conquer this spirit of death and all of its vicious weapons against me. I will gain my strength to overcome these fears by the strength found in the promises of God's Word, amen.

Group Discussion

With your group, discuss the things you are most afraid of, and brainstorm together about steps you can take to overcome. Group leader, caution the group not to laugh and embarrass anyone dealing with fear. The purpose of this group discussion is to be honest, as truth sets us free, and help each other to address fears and overcome them. You will discover how fearful God's people have become. It's time to be free from it, in the name of Jesus.

LONELINESS

Like fear, loneliness is another partner of the spirit of death, and it causes people to pull away from others. And this is what the enemy wants—he wants to isolate us and make us think we are all alone in this battle. But this is when we need to encourage ourselves in the faith that God cares. He understands what we are going through. Hebrews 4:15-16 (AMP) shares why Jesus understands what we are suffering through and why:

> *For we do not have a High Priest who is unable to sympathize and understand our weaknesses and temptations, but One who has been tempted [knowing exactly how it feels to be human] in every respect as we are, yet without [committing any] sin. Therefore let us [with privilege] approach the throne of grace [that is, the throne of God's gracious favor] with confidence and without fear, so that we may receive mercy [for our failures] and find [His amazing] grace to help in time of need [an appropriate blessing, coming just at the right moment].*

Something hurtful has happened to you, and it causes you to withdraw from people, and the results of pulling away is that you feel lonelier than you did before. What's causing this loneliness? Perhaps, you are being attacked with sickness and disease and lack the physical strength to be with people. Maybe you lost a loved one and are struggling to heal from the real pain of grief. Or you may have been betrayed by a spouse or close friend. There are many reasons why you can feel all alone at times, and it is difficult to pick up the broken pieces and move forward again. But with Jesus there is hope to overcome loneliness.

Trials come to all of us, and they often make us feel fearful and lonely. Jesus experienced loneliness the night He was arrested and during the suffering of Calvary, when those closest to Him deserted

Him because they feared being seen with Him would cause them harm, even possible death. And when He transformed into the curse to redeem us from it, He felt the ultimate loneliness—separation from His heavenly Father so we would never have to know this loneliness: *"...My God, My God, why have You forsaken Me?"* (Matthew 27:46).

If you feel lonely now, call upon the name of Jesus. He understands the pain of what you are suffering. He promises to never leave or forsake you, see Hebrews 13:5. If this is where you are in life right now, I encourage you to spend time with the Lord every day and meditate upon the following Scriptures, allowing the healing process to begin. Reach out to Him with a true desire to heal from loneliness.

Tell Him, "Jesus, I sense a real lack of support during this time of need in my life. Help me to see that my help comes from You. *"The man of too many friends [chosen indiscriminately] will be broken in pieces and come to ruin, but there is a [true, loving] friend who [is reliable and] sticks closer than a brother"* (Proverbs 18:24 AMP). Thank You, Jesus, because You are my true Friend, and I desire to come into close fellowship with You."

Ask Him to help you:

Holy Spirit, help me to be patient with myself and those around me, and to remember Your promise in Psalm 147:3 (AMP), "He heals the brokenhearted and binds up their wounds [healing their pain and comforting their sorrow]." I give You my brokenness, pain, and sorrow. I receive Your comfort during this time of great pain. I accept Your healing balm of Gilead into my mind and emotions. And I confess with my mouth that I may have lost someone or something very dear to me, but I am not lost. You found me. I am not without hope, for You are the hope of my salvation. I am not alone, because You will never leave me. I am loved by You, and Your love is unconditional toward me. You care about me, and provide for my every need. You heal me and make me whole in spirit, soul, and in body. With Your help, I will meditate upon these promises found in Your holy Scriptures. I will see that I am not alone and this spirit of heaviness, of loneliness will lift off me. In Jesus' name, I pray, amen.

Remember, Jesus is your Lord and High Priest, and He understands the pain of abandonment and loneliness, and He also knows the pathway to healing a broken heart. Reach out to Him, trust Him. He's not left your side, He's with you. Call out to Him by faith, and let Him hold you tight until the fear and loneliness pass.

Four Ways to Help Heal Loneliness

1. Reach out to God and to people around you.
2. Get involved with the activities at your local church or community.
3. Pay close attention to your thoughts—don't think negatively about yourself and others.
4. And remember, loneliness is an emotion, a feeling, not a fact.

Prayer

Dear Holy Spirit,

Help me to take this message to heart. Gently remind me when I feel all alone that I am not—You are with me. It doesn't matter where I find myself today, I know You are with me, and You care about me. You are my true Friend, and You stick with me through good and bad times. You promise to heal my broken heart, bind up my wounds, heal me of this pain, and comfort me in times of sorrow. And this brings comfort to my heart. Thank You, Holy Spirit. In Jesus' name, amen.

Pledge

> I pledge this day to God and to myself that I will receive the comfort of the Holy Spirit in my life. I will accept His supernatural healing ointment within my mind and emotions. I will receive His gentle reminders that I am never alone—He is always with me. I surrender this lonely heart to Him, and allow Him entrance to the secret places of my heart so that He can bind up my wounds, heal me of pain, and comfort me in times of sorrow.

Group Discussion

In a safe environment, have a heart-to-heart talk about loneliness. Openly discuss the cause of it in the life of your group members. Freely discuss the four ways to heal loneliness, and how you can better support one another in this.

DISCOURAGEMENT

Discouragement is yet another partner to the spirit of death. And it's a strong weapon the enemy will use against you—beware of its attachment to death itself. Are you fighting discouragement?

A lady wrote me the other night with the following need for prayer for a miracle. She shared, "My cancer returned after three years and I feel so bad. I am going to undergo radiation and chemo in the next few days. I need prayer. Please, I need help to get new cells and lymph nodes, and complete healing and removal of all cancer cells in my body."

This sister in the Lord received a negative medical report, and naturally discouragement follows right behind the negative words of "cancer returns." And so too the spirit of fear floods her memories of the pain she experienced years ago with all the radiation and chemo treatments and procedures. Knowing she needs help to overcome this discouragement and the deadly attack against her life, she does the right thing and reaches out to someone who will encourage her in the faith to stand strong on the promise of God's Word, *"by His stripes she is healed,"* see Isaiah 53:4-5.

Perhaps, you are in a similar situation as this woman and need help to get out of the realm of discouragement and find someone who will offer hope to trust God for a miracle. If so, you are not alone; many struggle to find a bit of encouragement these days. Let's face it, the news is gloomy, social media is filled with hate, and in general, people have become so negative.

So, where do God's people find a word of hope? Right from the Source—God's Word. And this is where we are going to turn to right now and search the Scriptures to fight off discouragement.

Let's begin with a prayer directly to the Source of encouragement: *"From the ends of the earth I call to you, I call as my heart grows faint; lead me to the rock that is higher than I"* (Psalm 61:2 NIV).

Psalm 27:14 gives us biblical instruction on how to overcome discouragement: *"Wait on the Lord; be of good courage, and He shall strengthen your heart; wait, I say, on the Lord!"* We are to wait on the Lord with hope, with expectancy, like a pregnant woman awaits the blessed day for the birth of her child.

Consider the word "wait" in a different manner, not just as a period of time passing by waiting for something to happen, but to wait to serve the Lord. Look at this well-known verse from Isaiah 40:31 in this way, *"But those who wait on the Lord shall renew their strength; they shall mount up with wings like eagles, they shall run and not be weary, they shall walk and not faint."*

As we serve the Lord with a true heart, our strength is renewed. We are filled with joy; and because joy is a supernatural strength, we become stronger as we serve Him. And to clarify what I mean by serving the Lord, it doesn't mean to take on another task at your local place of fellowship, but to wait upon Him as follows:

Four Steps to Find Your Source of Encouragement

1. **Believe God**. In the Gospel according to John, our beloved Jesus comforts us with His words in John 14:1, *"Let not your heart be troubled; you believe in God, believe also in Me."*

2. **Worship Him in spirit and in truth**. Jesus tells us in John 4:24, *"God is Spirit, and those who worship Him must worship in spirit and truth."*

3. **Pray in the Spirit and encourage yourself**. Apostle Paul instructs us in First Corinthians 14:4 (NIV) how to encourage ourselves. He says, *"Anyone who speaks in a tongue edifies themselves, but the one who prophesies edifies the church."*

4. **Perfect the love of God in you by His Word**. Apostle John writes to us in First John 2:5 (NIV), *"But if anyone obeys his word, love for God is truly made complete in them. This is how we know we are in him."*

If you follow these simple steps, you will find your Source of encouragement in Christ and overcome the enemy's power of discouragement.

Prayer

Dear Holy Spirit,

When I feel discouraged, I ask You for the spiritual strength to do what I know I need to do to break through to the realm of encouragement. Help me to still my heart before You, to open my mouth and worship You in spirit and in truth, to remember to pray in my heavenly language, to fellowship with You in Your Word, and to sit still and be quiet and just listen to You speak

Your words of encouragement to my heart. Thank You for Your
help, in Jesus' name, I pray, amen.

Pledge

I pledge with all my heart to God and to myself that I will
take hold of God's message of encouragement. I see that it is
His joy that gives me strength for today and hope for tomor-
row. I will not dwell on the past, but I will go to the Rock
that is higher than I, and wait upon Him, and worship Him
in spirit and in truth. And as I do, discouragement will pass
and encouragement will reign in my heart.

Group Discussion

As a group, discuss different ways you can encourage one another.
Together you can come up with a plan of action. Perhaps, you can
pair individuals to be accountable to one another. I would encourage
you to refrain from gifts and keep this in the realm of true, heartfelt word exchange. This is what people need the most when they are
facing discouragement.

DEPRESSION

Depression has a strong link to the spirit of death. Like any other emotion, it can come upon anyone, but it's a problem when it lingers. I
believe it lingers when we live in the emotional realm of past hurts and
disappointments. Reliving the painful moment over and over again is a
trap of the enemy to bring us down to his level of defeat where he can
easily cause further harm.

Reliving the pain of the past is like a cow regurgitating its food. It
keeps coming back up. The enemy will use the pain of the past against
us if we allow him to—don't! Next time satan brings up these hurtful
memories of the past, spit the memories out, tell the devil to leave you

alone, and to be silent, because you are not going to chew on the cud of his negativity any longer.

Depression is a pressing down of the spirit, it lowers the ability of the soul, the mind, and the emotions to carry us through life's situations. It prevents the supernatural strength of joy to lift us up to higher ground with Jesus. It drains energy and strength from our entire being. It's a life-stopper. Very troublesome things happen to everyone in this life, but it doesn't mean we have to live in a depressed state forever.

Some Facts about Depression[1]

- Depression affects 20-25% of Americans ages 18+ in a given year. (CDC)
- Depression is the leading cause of disability worldwide.
- Females experience depression at roughly two times the rate of men. (SMH)

There is hope to overcome depression—Jesus. Psalm 40:1-3 (NIV) tells us,

> *I waited patiently for the Lord; he turned to me and heard my cry. He lifted me out of the slimy pit, out of the mud and mire; he set my feet on a rock and gave me a firm place to stand. He put a new song in my mouth, a hymn of praise to our God. Many will see and fear the Lord and put their trust in him.*

When I read these words, *"He lifted me out of the slimy pit, out of the mud and mire,"* I get this image in my mind's eye of a pit filled with quicksand and someone stuck in the middle of it. The more the person tries to get out in their own strength, the farther they sink. It's a frustrating place to be because no matter what, the person continues to sink.

In order to escape this pit of sinking sand, you have to remain calm and still and allow someone to come and pull you out—rescue you. This is what Jesus, the Rock of our Salvation does for us. He extends His hand; and at that moment we have a choice to make: grab hold of it or reject His help.

When we take hold of Him, He lifts us up out of the mud and the mire and places us on a solid foundation—the Rock of our Salvation, His redemptive work.

For those sinking in a deep pit of depression, Jesus extends His hand toward them—to you—this day. He waits patiently for you to grab hold of His hand so He can place you on the Rock, His plan of salvation. Included in this plan of salvation are a host of benefits for you to accept and apply to life. The following are five of these benefits to ponder:

1. **Forgiveness.** Apostle Paul writes to us in Ephesians 1:7 (NIV), *"In him we have redemption through his blood, the forgiveness of sins, in accordance with the riches of God's grace."*

2. **Eternal Life.** Jesus, our Redeemer, promises us, *"For God so loved the world that He gave His only begotten Son, that whoever believes in Him should not perish but have everlasting life"* (John 3:16).

3. **A New Beginning.** Again the apostle Paul gives us a message of hope in Second Corinthians 5:17, *"Therefore, if anyone is in Christ, he is a new creation; old things have passed away; behold, all things have become new."*

4. **Acceptance into His Family.** Paul, an apostle of Christ, explains to us about our acceptance into God's family, *"In other words, it is not the children by physical descent who are God's children, but it is the children of the promise who are regarded as Abraham's offspring"* (Romans 9:8 NIV).

5. **Unconditional Love.** The Word of the Lord in Jeremiah 31:3 (NIV) encourages us with these endearing words, *"...I have loved you with an everlasting love; I have drawn you with unfailing kindness."*

Prayer

Dear Holy Spirit,

I need Your help to be free from this lingering depression. I do not desire to relive the pain of the past anymore. I desire to pass through the healing process with Your help. I thank You for Your forgiveness, Your unconditional love, acceptance into Your family, a new beginning, and eternal life with You—free from depression, in Jesus' name I pray, amen.

Pledge

I pledge to God and to myself to take the necessary steps to be free from lingering depression. I make a quality decision with the help of my Lord and Savior, Jesus Christ, to let go of the past and move forward in the power of God's forgiveness, His unconditional love, and His acceptance of me. Today is a new day, a brand-new beginning, and I move forward with the strength of His joy. I hold on to His hope for my future, amen.

Group Discussion

Start a group discussion about depression. Ask if someone will briefly share a time when the person had to fight off depression. Discuss the five benefits listed from the Plan of Salvation that can help refocus people from depression and defeat to freedom in Jesus.

ANXIETY

Another partner that the spirit of death will use to latch onto you is through anxiety. Do you struggle with anxiety and panic attacks? Do you feel overwhelmed? Does your world feel like it's caving in on all sides at once? Look to Jesus. He's the author and finisher of your faith (Hebrews 12:2). He will never leave you, or forsake you (Hebrews 13:5).

God's not angry like the world would have you believe Him to be. Psalm 86:15 (AMP) beautifully describes the goodness of God toward us, *"But You, O Lord, are a God [who protects and is] merciful and gracious, slow to anger and abounding in lovingkindness and truth."* If you allow Him, He protects you, Second Thessalonians 3:3 (AMP) says it like this, *"But the Lord is faithful, and He will strengthen you [setting you on a firm foundation] and will protect and guard you from the evil one."*

Sometimes we can feel overwhelmed because we focus on the problem, and in doing so we wind up magnifying our enemy, the devil. When in reality, the things he whispers to us are just lies. In John 8:44, Jesus calls him the father of all lies. The devil takes the Scriptures and twists them, and he makes his lies believable to us; once we grab hold of his lies, then they can produce in our life. We are reminded by the words of God in Isaiah 41:10, *"Fear not, for I am with you; be not dismayed, for I am your God. I will strengthen you, yes, I will help you, I will uphold you with My righteous right hand."* We need to think about what we are dwelling upon—the promises of God or the lies of the devil.

When you feel the negative reports or circumstances are too much to bear, and you feel anxiety try to take control of your mind and emotions, slip away to a quiet place with the Lord. This does not need to be a physical place, but a spiritual one. You are instructed in Matthew 6:6 (NIV), *"But when you pray, go into your room, close the door and pray to your Father, who is unseen. Then your Father, who sees what is done in secret, will reward you."*

The Bible tell us to, *"Be anxious for nothing, but in everything by prayer and supplication, with thanksgiving, let your requests be made known to God; and the peace of God, which surpasses all understanding, will guard your hearts and minds through Christ Jesus"* (Philippians 4:6-7).

Be honest with Him and confess this weakness, this sin of anxiety. Say to Him, "Lord, I know that I am not to be worried, but sometimes I am, and especially now. Help me to deal with each and every one of my concerns, and to take into account all that You have promised me, and to remember that You care for me. I ask this in Your name, amen."

I have come to the realization over and over again that the more time I spend with God, the safer I feel in the security of His loving arms. And I encourage you, the next time you feel overwhelmed by life, choose instead to think about the following:

1. Focus on the love Jesus has for you.

2. Contemplate upon His mercy that He feels for you.

3. Take comfort in the fact that He wills to protect you.

4. Spend time with Him in prayer until His peace takes over in you.

Prayer

Dear Holy Spirit,

I ask for Your help to overcome this anxiety controlling my mind and emotions. I desire to be free from this and walk in the peace of God that surpasses all understanding. Remind me with Your gentle nudge when I am entering into the realm of anxiety. I know that all things are possible with You, and I can't do this without You. Thank You for being with me to help me walk in victory over anxiety, in the name of Jesus I pray, amen.

Pledge

I pledge to God and to myself to work with the Holy Spirit to overcome the sin of anxiety in my life. I promise to follow His leading and to rest in His provision and power in my life. For the glory of God, amen.

HOW TO REACH OUT AND HELP

As a friend or loved one, how can I help someone who is fighting with negative emotions that are out of control such as fear, loneliness, discouragement, depression, anxiety, and other harmful emotions without becoming a victim of those I am trying to help?

1. Know that you can't force someone to overcome negative emotions if they don't want to be free from them.

2. Be sincere in your support.

3. Give a listening ear.

4. Pray for them.

5. Encourage them with hopeful reminders that this is a season in their life and with help it can pass, as long as they are willing to do their part and accept help.

6. Offer reasonable help, without being controlled by them.

7. Don't become an enabler; they are responsible for their own actions.

8. Suggest an intervention.

9. Offer to take them to their first session with a local pastor who is known to help people in the community, or a doctor, or support group.

In the next chapter we are going to study to understand spiritual forces better. Why does God care about us? Why is satan against us? And learn about angels and demons and what part do they play in this battle.

Prayer

> *Dear Holy Spirit,*
>
> *I have seen how I have allowed negative feelings like fear, loneliness, discouragement, depression, and anxiety get the best of me at times. I repent from holding on to a spirit of fear instead of surrendering to You, Holy Spirit. Forgive me for believing the lies of the enemy that no one cares about me. I know You care for me and will not abandon me. I confess that I have allowed depression to linger. I now see what I need to do to be free from this oppression. I ask You to forgive me for not casting my cares upon You and for allowing worry to take over my mind and emotions and control my life. I thank You, Holy Spirit, that You are my Comforter. I rely upon Your great strength to conquer these negative feelings and overthrow the spirit of death in my life. In Jesus' name I pray, amen.*

Pledge

I make a pledge, a promise to God and myself to seal the door against the spirit of death. I will not to allow it entrance into my life by its partners of fear, loneliness, discouragement, depression, anxiety, and mind-altering drugs. I will use godly wisdom and guard the door of my heart for the sake of my life and well-being.

After reading this chapter, we have a better understanding how negative emotions such as fear, loneliness, discouragement, depression, and anxiety in the beginning may seem harmless, but in reality quickly form partnerships with the spirit of death and create utter havoc in our lives. Therefore, we've taken measures to biblically protect ourselves from allowing these spiritual partners to take us down the wrong pathway that can lead us to premature death.

Questions for Chapter 2—Negative Emotions Partner with the Spirit of Death

1.   What do most people fear the most?

2.   What spirit is the forerunner for the spirit of death?

3.   Why does the enemy want you to feel lonely?

4.   Discouragement has a strong attachment to what?

5.   What are five steps to find your Source of encouragement?

6.   When is depression a problem?

7.   How can depression linger?

8.   Why do we feel overwhelmed at times?

9.   What does the devil whisper to you?

Personal Reflection

As I reflect on the message of this chapter, am I struggling with any negative emotions like fear, loneliness, discouragement, depression, or anxiety? Do I need to reach out to another person for help? If so, to whom can I reach out?

Group Discussion

We've discussed the connection of negative feelings such as fear, loneliness, discouragement, depression, and anxiety and how quickly they can link us to the spirit of death. We've shared from our hearts about the areas that we struggle with. Now talk about what we have learned from our study in this chapter to guard our hearts from these negative feelings and not let them get control of our mind and emotions and open the door for the spirit of death to enter. And how to reach out and help our loved ones without becoming the victim ourselves.

ENDNOTE

1. SAVE (Suicide Awareness Voices of Education), https://save.org/about-suicide/suicide-facts/; accessed May 27, 2019.

Chapter 3

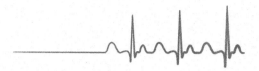

UNDERSTANDING SPIRITUAL FORCES AND ACTIVITIES

WORD OF THE LORD

The Lord Your God would say to you this day, "I am what I say I am. I am the God of your salvation. I am the Way, the Truth, and the Life. I am your hope in the time of need, I am your grace, I am your justice, I am your righteousness. I love you with an unconditional love that is based upon Me, and not upon your deeds—whether they be good or bad. I change not. My thoughts concerning you remain the same—precious in every way. Learn to lean on Me and not upon your limited understanding. Come to Me all you who are weary and heavy laden and I will give you rest. My plans for you are the best, and My purposes are to prosper you in spirit, soul, and body."

TWO SUPERNATURAL FORCES

There are two supernatural forces in this battle, the most powerful being is God—God the Father, God the Son Jesus Christ, and God the Holy Spirit. God will always be the Giver of Life, both eternal life and abundant life on this earth. As the Creator, everything He does creates and supports life—now and forever. We read in John 4:24 (AMP), *"God is spirit [the Source of life, yet invisible to mankind]...."*

Scriptures about Eternal Life

- In the Gospel of John, Jesus reassures us with these words about everlasting life, *"For God so loved the world that He gave His only begotten Son, that whoever believes in Him should not perish but have everlasting life"* (John 3:16).

- Paul writes in his letter to the Romans that eternal life is a gift, *"For the wages of sin is death, but the gift of God is eternal life in Christ Jesus our Lord"* (Romans 6:23).

- In John's Gospel, Jesus gives us this assuring promise concerning eternal life, *"And I give them eternal life, and they shall never perish; neither shall anyone snatch them out of My hand"* (John 10:28).

Scriptures about Abundant Life on Earth

- In John 10:10, Jesus says about Himself, *"...I have come that they may have life, and that they may have it more abundantly."*

- The Apostle of Love, John prays, *"Beloved, I pray that you may prosper in all things and be in health, just as your soul prospers"* (3 John 2:1).

- In the second letter of Paul to the Corinthians he writes, *"And God is able to make all grace abound toward you, that you, always having all sufficiency in all things, may have an abundance for every good work"* (2 Corinthians 9:8).

WHY DOES GOD CARE ABOUT US?

We might ask ourselves, *Why does God care that we have both eternal life and live in abundance while on this earth?* The answer to this question is actually quite simple, and yet at the same time it's very profound and deeply changes us for the better.

Despite all of our failures and imperfections—He loves us. The reason for this love has to do with His character and nature. And this is worth checking into.

The first part of the Godhead is the Creator, and we are His creation, His children. He is the loving Father who gave to us His best gift—His Son, who is the second part of the Godhead, Jesus Christ. Jesus is the Savior, and He gave to us all that He could, His life. And by the power of His blood that He freely offered on our behalf at Calvary, along with eternal life, we can receive His forgiveness and His healing for our spirit (our eternal being), our soul (the mind and the emotions), and for our physical bodies too. This same Son, Yeshua, is also known as the Good Shepherd who watches over us and attends to our needs well.

The third part of the Godhead is the Holy Spirit; He is our Comforter. He hovers overs us with the supernatural power of God to release the miraculous in our lives. God's DNA is love, and it's His nature to cherish, to love dearly His creation—us.

In the Book of Lamentations, the weeping prophet Jeremiah cries out, *"It is because of the Lord's lovingkindnesses that we are not consumed, because His [tender] compassions never fail. They are new every morning; great and beyond measure is Your faithfulness"* (Lamentations 3:22-23 AMP).

In the Psalm of David concerning the Lord's mercy, we read this song of praise, *"The Lord is merciful and gracious, slow to anger and abounding in compassion and lovingkindness"* (Psalm 103:8 AMP).

In Paul's letter to the Romans we read this important spiritual fact, *"But God clearly shows and proves His own love for us, by the fact that while we were still sinners, Christ died for us"* (Romans 5:8 AMP).

The loving apostle John writes to us in his first letter about the quality of the Father's love and the benefit we receive from His love, *"See what an incredible quality of love the Father has shown to us, that we would [be permitted to] be named and called and counted the children of God! And so we are! For this reason the world does not know us, because it did not know Him"* (1 John 3:1 AMP).

From the first letter of John we learn about the love connection and God, *"The one who does not love has not become acquainted with God [does not and never did know Him], for God is love. [He is the originator of love, and it is an enduring attribute of His nature]"* (1 John 4:8 AMP).

Then we have our enemy, satan, who is the lesser being of the two supernatural powers. God created him as a beautiful angel named lucifer, but he became sinful, and full of pride. He deceived himself and one-third of the angels with him, and they rebelled against God and tried to dethrone Him. Because of his foolish and wicked pride, they were evicted from Heaven, cast away from the holy presence of God. He is now referred to as satan, the devil. He is a fallen angel.

In the Book of Isaiah, the Hebrew prophet, Isaiah writes about the fall of lucifer.

> *How you are fallen from heaven, O Lucifer, son of the morning! How you are cut down to the ground, you who weakened the nations! For you have said in your heart: "I will ascend into heaven, I will exalt my throne above the stars of God; I will also sit on the mount of the congregation on the farthest sides of the north; I will ascend above the heights of the clouds, I will be like the Most High." Yet you shall be brought down to Sheol, to the lowest depths of the Pit. Those who see you will gaze at you, and consider*

you, saying: "Is this the man who made the earth tremble, who shook kingdoms, who made the world as a wilderness and destroyed its cities, who did not open the house of his prisoners?" All the kings of the nations, All of them, sleep in glory, Everyone in his own house; but you are cast out of your grave like an abominable branch, like the garment of those who are slain, thrust through with a sword, who go down to the stones of the pit, like a corpse trodden underfoot. You will not be joined with them in burial, because you have destroyed your land and slain your people. The brood of evildoers shall never be named. Prepare slaughter for his children because of the iniquity of their fathers, lest they rise up and possess the land, and fill the face of the world with cities. (Isaiah 14:12-21).

In the Book of Ezekiel, written by the Hebrew prophet Ezekiel, we read why lucifer was kicked out of Heaven:

By the abundance of your trading you became filled with violence within, and you sinned; therefore I cast you as a profane thing out of the mountain of God; and I destroyed you, O covering cherub, from the midst of the fiery stones. Your heart was lifted up because of your beauty; you corrupted your wisdom for the sake of your splendor; I cast you to the ground, I laid you before kings, that they might gaze at you. You defiled your sanctuaries by the multitude of your iniquities, by the iniquity of your trading; therefore I brought fire from your midst; it devoured you, and I turned you to ashes upon the earth in the sight of all who saw you. All who knew you among the peoples are astonished at you; you have become a horror, and shall be no more forever (Ezekiel 28:16-19).

In the apostle John's revelation, he records how Michael, the archangel with his warring angels overpower the devil, also known as satan: *"So the great dragon was cast out, that serpent of old, called the Devil and Satan, who deceives the whole world; he was cast to the earth, and his angels were cast out with him"* (Revelation 12:9).

THE CHARACTER AND NATURE OF SATAN

In the Gospel of John, Jesus tells us about the core nature of the devil, and why he is not to be trusted. He blatantly tells us that he is a murderer, a liar, and the father of all lies (see John 8:44).

Again by the descriptive words of Jesus about the devil, He reveals what satan is and what his intentions against us are. He says that satan is our enemy, and a thief, and that he only comes to steal, to kill, and to destroy (see John 10:10).

The apostle Peter warns us about the devil saying that he walks about like a roaring lion, seeking someone to devour (see First Peter 5:8).

The devil is against God, against us, against life, both eternal life and abundant life on this earth, and in no way wants to see us prosper and be in good health. He is bent upon our destruction and devises wicked plans to steal, to kill, and to destroy us.

We read in Luke 13:15-16, in regard to the woman who had a spirit of infirmity for eighteen years, that Jesus sternly rebuked the synagogue official and made it clear who was responsible for this woman's suffering, *"The Lord then answered him and said, 'Hypocrite! Does not each one of you on the Sabbath loose his ox or donkey from the stall, and lead it away to water it? So ought not this woman, being a daughter of Abraham, whom Satan has bound—think of it—for eighteen years, be loosed from this bond on the Sabbath?'"* The one who did this to her was satan.

Why does he hate us? Because we are created in the mirror image of the Father, Son, and Holy Spirit, and he is not.

Then God said, "Let Us make man in Our image, accord-ing to Our likeness; let them have dominion over the fish of the sea, over the birds of the air, and over the cattle, over all the earth and over every creeping thing that creeps on the earth." So God created man in His own image; in the image of God He created him; male and female He cre-ated them. Then God blessed them, and God said to them, "Be fruitful and multiply; fill the earth and subdue it; have dominion over the fish of the sea, over the birds of the air, and over every living thing that moves on the earth" (Genesis 1:26-28).

The devil also hates us because we have been given all authority over him: *"Behold, I give you the authority to trample on serpents and scorpi-ons, and over all the power of the enemy, and nothing shall by any means hurt you"* (Luke 10:19). He is jealous of people because our eternal des-tination has the potential of being in God's presence for eternity, if we make the right decision and become born again. In John 3:3 (NIV), Jesus says, *"Very truly I tell you, no one can see the kingdom of God unless they are born again."*

Whereas, the devil's eternal destination is recorded in Revelation 20:10: *"The devil, who deceived them, was cast into the lake of fire and brimstone where the beast and the false prophet are. And they will be tor-mented day and night forever and ever."* This is a good Scripture to use when he tries to torment you. He fears his destination, and does not like to be reminded of it.

His pride and deception cost him everything—he lost it all. And this fallen angel wants to bring as many as he can with him. And if he can't deceive us to come with him, he will try to make life on this earth as miserable as he can for us. And this is the character and nature of our enemy.

Unlike the destructive force of satan, God has other created supernatural beings, that are loyal to Him—angels. And since the creation of people, they are sent on missions by God to help us. He calls them "ministering spirits." We will have a discussion about them in this next section.

ANGELS—GOD'S MINISTERING SPIRITS

God has angelic troops to assist us in this battle. Hebrews 1:14 (NIV) tells us concerning these angels, *"Are not all* angels *ministering spirits sent to serve those who will inherit salvation?"* These ministering spirits are sent by God to: deliver divine messages, reveal God's plans and truths, warn of imminent dangers, help us to escape disasters, make war against the devil and his demons, help us fight battles, frustrate the enemy's plans, open and close doors, and help us in many other ways too. They are God's ministering spirits that assist us as He commands.

Angels Deliver Divine Messages from God

Angels are summoned to deliver divine messages from God as we see in Genesis 18. Three such angels visit Abraham to personally tell him that Sarah, his wife, will bear a promised son in her old age. And it comes to pass just as they said.

In Luke 1, Zacharias is visited by God's ministering spirit, the angel Gabriel. He declares to him that his barren wife, Elizabeth, will have a son in her old age, and he is to call him John. Later this same angel, Gabriel, appears to Mary, a young virgin, and delivers a divine message from God that she will give birth to the long-awaited Messiah. In Luke 2, we read how he then appeared to a group of shepherds in the field to announce the birth of Christ, and then a multitude of angels appeared alongside him praising God for the birth of our Savior, Jesus.

Angels Are Sent to Reveal God's Plans and Truths

Angels are sent by God to reveal His plans to His people, it happens this way in Matthew 1:20, *"But while he thought about these things, behold, an angel of the Lord appeared to him in a dream, saying, 'Joseph, son of David, do not be afraid to take to you Mary your wife, for that which is conceived in her is of the Holy Spirit.'"*

Angels Are Sent to Give Divine Revelation

God sent His angel to reveal the end-time revelation to His beloved servant John, so he would write down all that he saw in scrolls to give to us: *"The Revelation of Jesus Christ, which God gave Him to show His servants—things which must shortly take place. And He sent and signified it by His angel to His servant John, who bore witness to the word of God, and to the testimony of Jesus Christ, to all things that he saw"* (Revelation 1:1-2).

Angels Warn of Imminent Danger

Angels are also sent by God to warn of imminent danger and give a plan of escape. Matthew 2:13-14 shares this angelic encounter with us: *"Now when they had departed, behold, an angel of the Lord appeared to Joseph in a dream and said, 'Arise, take the young Child and His mother, flee to Egypt, and stay there until I bring you word; for Herod will seek the young Child to destroy Him.' When he arose, he took the young Child and His mother by night and departed to Egypt,"*

Angels Are Sent to Help God's People Escape Disaster

Another example of how angels are sent to help us escape disaster can be found in Genesis 19:15-17 (ESV): *"As morning dawned, the angels urged Lot, saying, 'Up! Take your wife and your two daughters who are here, lest you be swept away in the punishment of the city.' But he lingered. So the men seized him and his wife and his two daughters by the hand, the Lord being merciful to him, and they brought him out and set him outside the city. And as they brought them out, one said, 'Escape for your life. Do not look back or stop anywhere in the valley. Escape to the hills, lest you be swept away.'"*

Angels Are Sent by God to Protect those Who Fear Him

Throughout the Scriptures we read how God sends angels out on His missions to protect His people. Psalm 34:7 (AMP) says, *"The angel of the Lord encamps around those who fear Him [with awe-inspired reverence and worship Him with obedience], and He rescues [each of] them."* In Exodus 14:19 (AMP), we see how these ministering angels are sent to protect God's people, *"The angel of God, who had been going before the camp of Israel, moved and went behind them. The pillar of the cloud moved from in front and stood behind them."* Psalm 91:11 tells us, *"For he will command his angels concerning you to guard you in all your ways."*

We read in Daniel 6:22 how God sent an angel into the den where Daniel was wrongly thrown and he shut the mouths of the lions all night to protect Daniel from harm.

Angels Minister Courage to the Discouraged

In Genesis 16 we read how an angel of the Lord appeared to Sarai's handmaiden, Hagar, in the desert and gave her an encouraging word, for she was discouraged by the rejection of her mistress, Sarai.

In Judges 6 an angel delivered a message of encouragement to the discouraged Gideon that he and his army would defeat their enemy as one man. And then confirmed this message with a supernatural sign and wonder so that Gideon knew that this messenger and its message were truly from God.

Angels Engage in War against Satan and Demons

> *And war broke out in heaven: Michael and his angels fought with the dragon; and the dragon and his angels fought, but they did not prevail, nor was a place found for them in heaven any longer. So the great dragon was cast*

out, that serpent of old, called the Devil and Satan, who deceives the whole world; he was cast to the earth, and his angels were cast out with him* (Revelation 12:7-9).

Angels Fight for God's People

Angels are released to help fight the battle for us, we see this in Genesis 19:10-11 (KJV): *"But the men put forth their hand, and pulled Lot into the house to them, and shut to the door. And they smote the men that were at the door of the house with blindness, both small and great: so that they wearied themselves to find the door."* Angels rescued Lot from harm's way—they shut the door so not only Lot but his family was protected as well, especially his daughters, and blinded the eyes of the evil men. This bought a little bit of time and allowed Lot and his family time to escape Sodom and Gomorrah. These ministering spirits are often referred to as warring angels.

Angels Frustrate the Enemy's Plans against Us

We see another encounter of warring angels take place in the Red Sea, as recorded in Exodus 14:25: *"And He took off their chariot wheels, so that they drove them with difficulty; and the Egyptians said, 'Let us flee from the face of Israel, for the Lord fights for them against the Egyptians.'"*

Angels Are Sent to Open and Shut Doors

Angels were sent to open the prison doors for the apostles in Acts 5:19, *"But the angel of the Lord by night opened the prison doors, and brought them forth"* (KJV).

Angels shut the door of Lot's house and did not allow the evil men to enter: *"But the men reached out their hands and pulled Lot into the house with them, and shut the door"* (Genesis 19:10).

There are many more examples of ministering spirits, God's angels sent to help us on this earth. But the point is to show you He has a host of ministering spirits at His disposal waiting to be dispatched to help us in our time of trouble. Allow God to send them your way.

WARNING: *We Do Not Worship Angels—We Worship God Only.*

The Bible clearly teaches us that we are not to worship angels. Remember they are created beings sent out by God on missions to help those who inherit salvation—us. It is important to note that this means in the spectrum of the supernatural that you are greater than angels. You have more authority than they do.

Oftentimes people, including God's people, make the mistake of worshipping angels. Only God is worthy to be praised. And we are given strict instructions in Exodus 20:3, the first of the Ten Commandments: "*You shall have no other gods before Me.*" In Matthew 4:10, Jesus rebukes satan and declares, "*You shall worship the Lord your God, and Him only you shall serve.*"

John, the author of Revelation, was rebuked when he bowed down to the angel that appeared to him in Revelation 19:9-10 (NIV): "*Then the angel said to me, 'Write this: Blessed are those who are invited to the wedding supper of the Lamb!' And he added, 'These are the true words of God.' At this I fell at his feet to worship him. But he said to me, 'Don't do that! I am a fellow servant with you and with your brothers and sisters who hold to the testimony of Jesus. Worship God! For it is the Spirit of prophecy who bears testimony to Jesus.'*" From this portion of Scripture, I would have to conclude that any angel that allows you to bow down and worship it is not of God, but a demon in disguise.

In the natural, we do not worship a servant or pray to a servant, they are given an order, a command, or given instructions to serve. It works the same way in the supernatural realm, but all through the Servant of servants—Jesus Christ.

Judge Them

Not only are we not to worship these ministering spirits, God's angels, but we are also given a warning in these last days that we are to test the spirits. Are they truly angels sent by God to minister help or are they fallen angels, demons, dressed in godly apparel to deceive us in these last days? Let's talk more about this in the next section.

DEMONS

Now let's examine the other supernatural force, demons. What are they? Where did they come from? What do they do? How do we label them?

The angels who fell with lucifer, now called satan or the devil, and were evicted from Heaven are now called demonic spirits, or demons—they are the fallen angels. Their leader is our enemy—satan, which makes them our enemy as well. They carry out the works of satan to steal from us, to kill us, and to destroy us.

In the beginning of this work I share in my opening testimony that as a young believer I did not understand about demons or the death, sickness, and disease they carried. But since then I have learned how to handle them when I confront them and their work in others.

Let's read an example of this in Luke 13:11-13 that clearly says, *"And behold, there was a woman who had a spirit of infirmity eighteen years, and was bent over and could in no way raise herself up. But when Jesus saw her, He called her to Him and said to her, 'Woman, you are loosed from your infirmity.' And He laid His hands on her, and immediately she was made straight, and glorified God."*

The word "spirit" in this portion of Scripture means a demon (Lexicon: Strong's G4151, pneuma). And the word "infirmity" means frailty: disease, infirmity, sickness, weakness (Lexicon: Strong's G769, astheneia).

In this Scripture reference and in the following one, we see that demons not only are responsible for these sicknesses and diseases, but they are labeled or called by the harm they do.

Jesus calls this demon that causes a boy to go into an epileptic seizure, an epileptic spirit:

When they came to the crowd, a man came up to him and, kneeling before him, said, "Lord, have mercy on my son, for he is an epileptic and he suffers terribly. For often he falls into the fire, and often into the water. And I brought him to your disciples, and they could not heal him." And Jesus answered, "O faithless and twisted generation, how long am I to be with you? How long am I to bear with you? Bring him here to me." And Jesus rebuked the demon, and it came out of him, and the boy was healed instantly (Matthew 17:14-18 ESV).

I have found this to be very helpful when ministering to people. It has helped to remove the spookiness of confronting demon activity while ministering.

I believe that demons carry and release sickness and disease in whatever form to people. They have a stronghold over an individual. We need to exercise our authority over the strongman, the demon. Decree by faith, a separation between them and the individual, such as:

In Jesus' name I renounce a spirit of death, I decree that this person is cut off, separated from the strongman of lung cancer, and the power behind this label of cancer. I curse every cancerous cell and tumor at its very seed, and command it to dry up at the roots, and die off and be eliminated from the body. I release the Spirit of Life, and the healing power of Holy Spirit to flow in and throughout all cells, tissues, organs and systems and declare them recreated and made whole for the glory of Jesus, amen and amen.

What would we call a demon that causes people to suffer great torment? A tormenting spirit.

What do we call a demon that hinders God's answers from reaching His people? A hindering spirit. How would we refer to a demon that is lying to someone? A lying spirit.

Therefore, a spirit of death is a demon spirit that provokes death—premature death. And as a reminder, the spirit of death is a demon, a very powerful one that is bent upon our destruction to provoke premature death in our physical bodies. It works with a team of demons such as a spirit of fear, a spirit of infirmity, and others too. You need to take your God-given authority over it in the all-powerful name of Jesus.

BEWARE—HEED THE WARNING

Beware, demons, like their leader, satan, are very cunning and deceptive. The Bible gives us clear warning that in the last days they will deceive many, even God's people if possible. They are capable of temporarily changing their filthy demonic attire for what they once wore before the fall, and appear to us in their heavenly, angelic apparel. Their wicked leader, satan, can change his wretched rags and appear as a beautiful angel of light, and so can his legions of demons. We need to heed the warnings and not believe everything that appears to us.

> *Beloved, do not believe every spirit, but test the spirits, whether they are of God; because many false prophets have gone out into the world. By this you know the Spirit of God: Every spirit that confesses that Jesus Christ has come in the flesh is of God, and every spirit that does not confess that Jesus Christ has come in the flesh is not of God. And this is the spirit of the Antichrist, which you have heard was coming, and is now already in the world. You are of God, little children, and have overcome them, because He who is in you is greater than he who is in the world. They are of the world. Therefore they speak as of the world,*

and the world hears them. We are of God. He who knows God hears us; he who is not of God does not hear us. By this we know the spirit of truth and the spirit of error (1 John 4:1-6).

Therefore, the question to ask an angel to know if it is of God or not is, "Did Jesus Christ come in the flesh?" If they can answer the question, then they are a true ministering spirit sent by God, and if not, cast it far from you.

I speak more on this matter in my book, *Greater Than Magic,* in Chapter 11, "Protection from Deception," pages 131-142.

ANGELIC FRACTIONS

While we are warned to have a watchful eye and be on the lookout against the attacks of the enemy, we can become *too* focused on the devil and his wicked works, which causes us to forget that greater is Jesus in us than he, satan, who is in the world. So, I think it would be a good idea to brush up on our angelic fractions.

The mathematical facts are as follows:

- The angels that remained faithful to God are two-thirds.
- Those that rebelled against God with the devil are one-third.

So not only is our enemy the lesser power of the supernatural, he and his flock of demons are fewer in number. And our God is greater than satan in every way. And greater is the number of God's host of ministering angels to aid us in our times of trouble.

We've learned about the spiritual forces and what they do—who helps us and who harms us and how they activate their works—good or bad. As mentioned in Chapter 1, the battles we find ourselves in are not fought in the physical realm, but in spiritual realm. And this particular battle against the spirit of death—premature death, in whatever form it takes—is won in the supernatural realm of faith as well. In the next chapter we learn what it takes to win.

Prayer

> *Dear Holy Spirit,*
>
> *Help me to mature in the faith, to spiritually understand and accept the love that You have for me. I need Your guidance to walk in Your lovingkindness, mercy, and grace. Help me to not fear my enemy, but take my authority over him and his wicked works. I thank You that You are the Giver of Life, and that I am born again and have eternal life with You. I ask for Your grace to walk in the abundant life that You have for me on this earth. In Jesus' name I pray, amen.*

Pledge

I pledge to God and to myself to be wise when dealing with supernatural beings. I will worship God only, not angels. I will protect myself and my family from the power of deception from the enemy. I will test the spirits, and ask them, "Did Jesus Christ come in the flesh?" If they can confidently answer me with a yes, then I will know they are sent by God to me. If they cannot give me a direct answer to this simple question, then I know they are demons and I will cast them away from my presence, in Jesus' name.

Questions for Chapter 3—Understanding Spiritual Forces and Activities

1. There are two supernatural forces. Who is the most powerful?

2. God is always what?

3. What type of life does He give?

4. As the Creator, how does God give and support life?

5. Who is the lesser being of the two supernatural powers?

6. What was his name before he fell?

7. Why did he fall into sin?

8. What were the consequences of his foolish attempt to dethrone God?

9. What are angels?

10. What are some of the ways these ministering spirits help us?

11. What happened when John bowed down to worship the angel in Revelation 19:9-10?

12. What can we conclude about John's experience when he bowed to worship this angel?

13. What are demons?

14. Who is the leader of demons?

15. What do they carry out?

Personal Reflection

As I read through this chapter, can I safely say without a shadow of a doubt that I am on the right side of the supernatural? Am I on God's team? Or have I been deceived and on the wrong side of the battle? Have I aligned myself with satan and his demons without even knowing it? If so, am I willing to correct this grave error?

> *Father God,*
>
> *I ask You to forgive me for all my sins, including all doubt and unbelief concerning You. Forgive me because I really did not know what I was doing. But now I see how wrong I have been. Thank You for being willing to forgive me and to love me. This*

day I make You my Savior, my Deliverer, and my Healer. In Jesus' name I pray, amen.

Group Discussion

How do I feel about what we've studied in this chapter about spiritual forces and what they do? Have I had an angelic intervention that I know about and am willing to share with the others in this group? Do I recognize the attack of the enemy and his demonic force in an area of my life? Am I willing to share what I see so that the others can learn from my experience?

Part Two

CREATED TO WIN AND CONQUER THE SPIRIT OF DEATH

Take heart! We have been created to win and to conquer the spirit of death. In Part Two we will also discuss how to encourage, pray, and activate our faith for ourselves and for others in the fierce battles against death itself.

Chapter 4

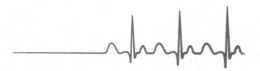

CREATED TO WIN

WORD OF THE LORD

The Lord God would say to you this day, "I created you to win. I filled you with My Holy Spirit deep within. The situation may look dim, the world may declare that the chance is slim, but even still, I created you to win. Don't look back, stay on track. I've got you covered; I bore this upon My back. And this healing you will not lack. I paid the fee, on the tree called Calvary, and from the enemy, you are free. If you will keep your eye on Me, you will see, you have the victory."

Did you know that you are created to win? And to win every battle that you face? When you become born again, you inherit the greater power within. This power is the Holy Spirit. He is the creative, explosive power of God. And He lives within your spirit—your spiritual temple.

> *But if the Spirit of Him who raised Jesus from the dead dwells in you, He who raised Christ from the dead will*

*also give life to your mortal bodies through His Spirit who
dwells in you* (Romans 8:11).

Wherever you go, He is with you. You were not created to lose to
satan, or to be pushed around and bullied by his wickedness. You were
created to overtake him by a simple command, *"Get behind me, Satan!"*
(See Matthew 4:10; 16:23.) You are created to be the head and not
the tail.

Why? Because Jesus crushed satan's head below His feet at Calvary.

> *And I will put enmity between you and the woman, and
> between your seed and her Seed; He shall bruise your head,
> and you shall bruise His heel* (Genesis 3:15).

Having said this, we sometimes need a reminder that there is no
sickness, no disease, or deadly attack of the enemy that is greater than
the power of the Holy Spirit. The only reason these attacks can suc-
ceed against us is that we allow them to—either because we do not
know how to fight to win, or we abandon hope, backing down from our
stance of faith and allowing the enemy to win the earthly battle.

WHAT DO WE NEED TO
FIGHT SUCCESSFULLY?

We're all soldiers in God's army. And we're in this battle together. When
one hurts, we all hurt. Let's consider what it takes to win this fight. As
God's soldiers, what do we need to fight successfully? We need:

1. A battle plan.

2. A vision that includes a reason to fight, a goal to
    achieve, and a reason to believe we can win.

3. To understand our spiritual rights to fight this battle
    successfully.

4. Weapons to fight with.

A Battle Plan

To fight this battle successfully, we need a battle plan. This plan needs to be clear and concise, and it needs to start with a vision. Proverbs 29:18 tells us that people perish for a lack of vision. In this vision we need to include a reason to fight, a goal to achieve, and a reason to believe you can win.

A Reason to Fight

Let's look at our reason to fight. A woman is sitting in the doctor's office. The doctors don't mince words with her; they are very upfront. The diagnosis is stage 4 breast cancer, and the prognosis is imminent death. She is told to put her affairs in order.

We've read the scenario, now for the conflict with the diagnosis and the prognosis. This woman is a Christian. She believes in the miracle-working power of the Lord. She is unwilling to give up and die. In this situation, she is well aware of her reason to fight—she has children and they need their mom.

I am not writing about a specific woman, but this is an all-too-common situation taking place in the lives of God's people today. To come up with an effective and successful battle plan, let's work with real-life situations that are happening today.

So in this story we see the woman's reason to fight—for the sake of her children. There are many other reasons, but this is first and foremost on the heart of this single mom.

What's your reason to fight this type of battle?

_____

_____

_____

_____

_____

_____

_____

A Goal to Achieve

The second part of creating this vision is to set a goal or goals to achieve. In this situation, the woman needs deliverance from a spirit of death and needs supernatural healing and creative miracles from Jesus. You may think this is too wild and out of touch with reality. But it depends upon the eye of the beholder, and what you are beholding. God gives you the choice to keep your eye on the hopeless report or turn to the Giver of Life—Jesus. This Christian woman decides to fix her eye on Jesus—her only hope.

> *I will lift up my eyes to the hills—from whence comes my help? My help comes from the Lord, who made heaven and earth* (Psalm 121:1-2).

And the truth of the matter is, this situation is out of control in the natural realm and has only one place to move to have victory—into the supernatural realm where healing and miracles happen to those who believe in the healing power of Jesus.

> *Now hope does not disappoint, because the love of God has been poured out in our hearts by the Holy Spirit who was given to us* (Romans 5:5).

Therefore, the woman's goals to achieve are deliverance from a spirit of death, supernatural healing from stage 4 breast cancer, and creative miracles for a strong and healthy, cancer-free body.

What are your goals to achieve in your fight to live?

_____

_____

_____

_____

_____

_____

_____

A Reason to Believe

The third part of this vision is to include a reason to believe you can win the battle. In this case, the woman can have a reason to believe—as long as she holds on to the revelation that with Jesus there is always hope. If she will remain hopeful, her faith can then be activated.

Let's find this reason to believe in God's Word—the standard for life on this earth and throughout eternity. What does it have to say about this woman's reason to believe?

- Prophet Isaiah foretold how our Jesus will suffer to heal people spiritually, emotionally, mentally and physically: *"But [in fact] He has borne our griefs, and He has carried our sorrows and pains; yet we [ignorantly] assumed that He was stricken, struck down by God and degraded and humiliated [by Him]. But He was wounded for our transgressions, He was crushed for our wickedness [our sin, our injustice, our wrongdoing]; the punishment [required] for our well-being fell on Him, and by His stripes (wounds) we are healed"* (Isaiah 53:4-5 AMP).

- Paul's letter to the Galatians reveals to us how Christ redeems us from the curse: *"Christ has redeemed us from the curse of the law, having become a curse for us (for it is written, 'Cursed is everyone who hangs on a tree'"* (Galatians 3:13).

- The great prophet Moses wrote down the words of God for us: *"...I am the Lord who heals you"* (Exodus 15:26).

From the Scriptures, what is your reason to believe you can win the battle?

_____

_____

_____

_____

_____

_____

Many people doubt God's healing power and are upset with those of us who do believe. I taught in my last work, *The Prophetic and Healing Power of Your Words*, that according to Proverbs 18:21 we have the power of life and death in our words. And instead of lining up our words with satan and his wicked works against this woman believing for a healing touch from Jesus, why not line them up with the redemptive blood of Jesus? Let's hang up the pink ribbon where it really belongs, on Jesus—He is our hope for healing!

OUR SPIRITUAL RIGHTS TO FIGHT THIS BATTLE

We know our reason to fight, we have our goal to achieve, and we even found our reason to believe. Now there is one more thing we should understand that will help us silence the doubts of the enemy. We have spiritual rights to win the battle. We have a blood covenant with the Father. And unique to a blood covenant is that it cannot be broken: *"Now may the God of peace who brought up our Lord Jesus from the dead, that great Shepherd of the sheep, through the blood of the everlasting covenant"* (Hebrews 13:20).

This blood covenant states in First John 5:14-15, *"Now this is the confidence that we have in Him, that if we ask anything according to His will, He hears us. And if we know that He hears us, whatever we ask, we know that we have the petitions that we have asked of Him."*

And we activate the blood covenant by our spiritual currency—faith: *"Now faith is the assurance (title deed, confirmation) of things hoped for (divinely guaranteed), and the evidence of things not seen [the conviction of their reality—faith comprehends as fact what cannot be experienced by the physical senses]"* (Hebrews 11:1 AMP).

So yes, this Christian woman has the spiritual rights to fight this battle. She has a blood covenant with the Father that can never be broken. She can be confident in knowing that if she asks anything according to His will, He hears her and she receives her healing. According to the many promises in God's Word, healing—whether spiritual, emotional, mental, or physical—is His will. Jesus shed His blood so that she can receive her much-needed deliverance from a spirit of death, healing from stage 4 breast cancer, and creative miracles for a healthy, strong, and cancer-free body. It is her spiritual right to fight this battle.

WHERE THE BATTLE IS REALLY WON

As a reminder from Chapter 1, "The Spirit of Death," Ephesians 6:12 tells us that the battles we find ourselves in are not fought in the physical realm against one another, but in the spiritual realm against evil spiritual beings.

> *We do not wrestle against flesh and blood, but against principalities, against powers, against the rulers of the darkness of this age, against spiritual hosts of wickedness in the heavenly places.*

You're in a battle, a tough one, but you have been graced with what it takes to win. Stand up and fight.

HAVING DONE ALL—STAND

> *Therefore take up the whole armor of God, that you may be able to withstand in the evil day, and having done all, to stand* (Ephesians 6:13).

So often God's people start to do all the right things and success in the battle begins to manifest. But then comes another fiery dart of the enemy and it takes them off guard. Their faith wanes, their countenance droops, and they retreat to the old negative feelings of defeat.

I received an email from an individual who I am coaching through their battle. Yesterday, the email was full of victory, but today the email is full of emotional defeat. I am not being hard-hearted here, just trying to make a point. You have to remain strong through the daily skirmishes; you cannot afford to give an inch of power over to the enemy in this fight. You dig your heels into the ground and you stand firm. Don't let him push you down. And if it should happen that you falter and fall, get right back up again.

This emotional up and down pattern is not helpful. Get off the emotional rollercoaster! Stand on the firm foundation of your faith—the redemptive blood of Jesus. We are created to win, not to give in to the attacks of the enemy. We are to take a stand, be unmovable, unshakable, and unstoppable. We are to mature in the faith and fight the enemy to the finish.

I understand what it is like to look death in the face and refuse to give in to it. When our son, Marcos, was lying in the incubator in the hospital, everything in the natural screamed death and hopelessness. It would have been so easy to just throw in the towel like we were being advised by everyone to do. But when you are created to win, you don't give up. You fight until you win. (To read about Marcos' testimony and how we raised him from the dead, see my book *DARE to Believe,* Chapter 11, pages 175-193.)

Even when trudging through the deep valleys of the battle, the Christian woman in this chapter's example can stand strong and remain firm in the faith with this declaration of faith, *"I shall not die, but live, and declare the works of the Lord"* (Psalm 118:17).

BE STRONG IN THE POWER OF HIS MIGHT

This particular battle against the spirit of death—premature death, in whatever form it takes—is won in the supernatural realm of faith. And the results of whether we win or lose the battle are clearly seen in the physical realm. That's why the apostle Paul encourages us in his letter to the Ephesians in 6:10 (NIV): *"Finally, be strong in the Lord and in his mighty power."*

Because this battle is spiritual, God does not expect us to rely on earthly measures, but in the power of His might. The Lord wants us to know that these battles are won *"not by might nor by power, but by My Spirit"* (Zechariah 4:6). It is so reassuring to know we are not on our own in this fight, and neither is the woman in our story.

How do we know if we are truly relying on the power of His might? I believe the answer to this question is whether or not we can hold on to our peace at the core of the battle. Even in the midst of a negative test result or a discouraging prognosis, we can hold our peace and know that God is still greater than what our ears are hearing, what our eyes are seeing, and what the enemy is bombarding our minds with. If our mind and emotions are not running away with us, but are at peace, I believe we are relying upon the power of His might.

PUT ON THE ARMOR OF GOD

God understands the battle we are in is not physical, but spiritual. And because it is a spiritual battle, He has given us supernatural weaponry to conquer our enemy, the devil, and his demonic force. He knows our enemy and his evil workings against us, and so should we. And He has equipped us with everything we need to overcome. Let's remind ourselves about the armor of God and what each piece of the armor is for. Let's train ourselves accordingly to have victory.

Ephesians 6:14 first mentions the Belt of Truth. This belt's makeup is God's truth. It keeps us in proper spiritual alignment. It protects us from the deceptive lies of the enemy. It keeps us honorable and upright in all of God's ways. God's truth also covers us with integrity, preventing us from being exposed to the world's sinful ways. John 8:32 shares with us what truth does for us, *"And you shall know the truth, and the truth shall make you free."*

As mentioned, truth is protective. And the truth of God's Word protects us from the spirit of death when it is activated, spoken out loud: *"Thou shalt come to thy grave in a full age, like as a shock of corn cometh in his season"* (Job 5:26 KJV).

Then we have the Breastplate of Righteousness to guard our hearts. In times of old, soldiers wore a breastplate to protect their hearts from fatal wounds. And spiritually speaking this is a very important piece of our spiritual armor to protect us from the ways of this world. This isn't just any breastplate, but a breastplate of righteousness. In and of ourselves we are not righteous, no matter how good we are or how many good works we accomplish. Our righteousness comes from the redemptive work of Jesus. Paul explains where our righteousness comes from in Second Corinthians 5:21:"*For He made Him who knew no sin to be sin for us, that we might become the righteousness of God in Him.*"

And in keeping with the theme of this work, *Conquering the Spirit of Death,* it's by the righteousness of Jesus that our sins and the consequences of those sins are not held against us. The Bible teaches us that the wages of sin are death (see Romans 6:23), but by this Breastplate of Righteousness, we can be delivered from a spirit of death—if we will believe in His righteousness.

Ephesians 6:15 talks about having our feet shod with the preparation of the gospel of peace. To do battle, a soldier must be prepared, and part of the attire back in these times were good sandals that would endure the rough terrain. To battle with our enemy victoriously, we must be prepared for the rough battles that lie ahead. Our preparedness comes from God's Word. Peace is the goal in any battle—peace with God, peace with other people, peace in our physical body, our marriage, with our finances...whatever that battle is, we must be prepared.

Make a declaration of faith that lines up with Isaiah 53:4-5, *"by His stripes I am healed"* and declare that this gospel of peace reigns in your mortal body—that every cell, tissue, organ, and system lines up to God's Word for the workings of a peaceful body.

Then we have in Ephesians 6:16, the Shield of Faith. With our faith in the redemptive blood of Jesus, we are able to quench, to put out all the fiery darts of the enemy. No matter what he throws at us, our faith is more powerful than he is.

Activate your faith against the attack from a spirit of death. With faith-filled words decree, declare, and confess the healing promises of

God over your body. Put your faith in action and align your actions with your words of faith.

Next, in Ephesians 6:17, we see we are to take the Helmet of Salvation. This is the most important piece of our armor. Without it we are eternally lost. As we look further into the meaning of salvation, we see that it comes from the Greek word *sōzō* (Strong's G4982), meaning to save, to heal, and to make whole. This includes healing of the spirit, soul (mind and emotions), and body.

Make sure you are in right standing with God; if you are not born again, receive Him as your Savior. If you need to repent of sin, do so. If you aren't where you should be spiritually, make things right with Him now.

Then we see mentioned in the list of our spiritual armor, the Sword of the Spirit. The Sword of the Spirit is the Word of God—the Bible. The Word of God is a most powerful weapon, especially when used under the leading of the Holy Spirit.

When Jesus was being tempted in the wilderness by the devil, He fought back and won every temptation by quoting the Word of God aloud to him. Do the same.

THE FULL ARMOR OF GOD

Put on the whole armor of God, that you may be able to stand against the wiles of the devil (Ephesians 6:11).

I find it interesting that the Word tells us that we are to put on the full armor of God, not just some of the armor, but all of it. And make no mistake, in order to win God's way, we need to dress ourselves with His armor. We need to be completely covered with His armor for the many battles we face, especially this one. And we are the ones responsible to dress ourselves. It's our decision whether we win or lose the battle. But remember, God created us to win and has given us everything needed to do so.

Activate Your Armor

Once we are fully dressed, then it's time to activate our armor so we can win. We can say, *"We believe,"* but until we put action behind our faith-filled words, we don't believe. Faith demands action. It always has, it always will. James says, *"For as the body without the spirit is dead, so faith without works is dead also"* (James 2:26). A lack of faith action demonstrates a heart that has not been changed. Your actions are proof that you believe.

FIGHT THE GOOD FIGHT OF FAITH

There are times in life when it just doesn't make any sense to believe God's promise. I'm sure when Moses and the Israelites were standing at the shores of the Red Sea and Pharaoh's army was bearing down hard upon them, it just didn't make sense. So the people panicked, started to complain, and wished they were back in Egypt.

Maybe you are facing a situation today that goes against human reasoning and common sense to trust in God's promises. The enemy is pursuing you with all his might, and the circumstance in front of you looks grim. So like the Israelites, you start to grumble, complain, and even doubt God's ability to rescue you.

That's how it was for the Israelites and that's how it can be for us when we allow circumstances to dictate our faith in the redemptive work of Jesus Christ.

Moses, the mighty man of God, cries out to the people in Exodus 14:13-14, *"Do not be afraid. Stand still, and see the salvation of the Lord, which He will accomplish for you today. For the Egyptians whom you see today, you shall see again no more forever. The Lord will fight for you, and you shall hold your peace."*

And this is all true and good, but God responds to Moses in a rather surprising way in verses 15-18, *"Why do you cry to Me? Tell the children of Israel to go forward. But lift up your rod, and stretch out your hand over the sea and divide it. And the children of Israel shall go on dry ground through the midst of the sea. And I indeed will harden the hearts of the Egyptians, and they shall follow them. So I will gain honor over Pharaoh and over all his army, his chariots, and his horsemen. Then the Egyptians shall know that I am the Lord, when I have gained honor for Myself over Pharaoh, his chariots, and his horsemen."*

God wants more than to rescue us, He wants us to strengthen our faith in Him, trust Him, move forward, and not just talk faith, but to actually live faith. He told Moses to put his faith into action, tell the people to move forward and while doing so he was to lift up his rod, stretch out his hand over the sea, and divide it for himself!

So often we want God to part the Red Sea that is in front of us, that separates us from entering the Promised Land, the miracle that we so desperately need. We, like Moses cry out and say, "God, part the waters for us!" And God responds, "No, you put your faith in Me into action, and according to your faith it will happen." God wills that we take responsibility, grow up in the faith, activate it, and part the Red Sea that is preventing us to enter into the Promised Land.

How do we do this?

1. **Empower our faith**. Strengthen our faith in the Word of God until we believe. If we need healing, we study healing until we believe it. Romans 10:17 reveals to us how faith comes: *"So then **faith comes by hearing, and hearing by the word of God.**"*

2. **Pray in tongues** to part our spiritual Red Seas. We pray in the Holy Spirit until we part the spiritual Red Sea that is hindering us from entering into the

Promised Land—God's realm of the supernatural where the miracles are waiting on us to be released: *"Likewise the Spirit also helps in our weaknesses. For we do not know what we should pray for as we ought, but the Spirit Himself makes intercession for us with groanings which cannot be uttered"* (Romans 8:26).

3. **Speak God's promises**. Speak aloud the promises of God concerning our situation. Proverbs 12:18 tells us, *"...the tongue of the wise promotes health."*

4. **Put faith into action**. Don't wait for God to do something; He already has at Calvary.

Now, it is up to us to activate the miraculous by our faith in His plan of atonement. James 1:22 says it like this, *"But be doers of the word, and not hearers only, deceiving yourselves."*

If we will take these four steps and work them until that spiritual Red Sea opens up for us, then we will be able to walk right on through and into the Promised Land, and activate the miracle we seek.

TESTIMONY OF VICTORY OVER PREMATURE DEATH

The following is a fabulous testimony of a man who heard the message of faith and healing, received prayer from our prayer team, and then worked his faith and overcame the spirit of death, and spoke a recreated heart into being.

Dear Becky, I have a praise report. I am totally healed. I had a bicuspid aortic valve. I was born with this as it is a heart defect formed in the womb. Normal people have tricuspid valves. I had an enlarged heart with damaged heart muscle. Today I have been cleared of all issues! I now have a tricuspid valve! My heart is correct size and no sign of damage. I spoke faith-filled words and told my heart to be healed three times a day. Glory to God. Thank You, Jesus. Thank You, Holy Spirit. –Tim from Upstate New York

This is true victory! He took on the spirit of death and defeated it. Like you, he is created to win. And win he did!

WORD OF THE LORD

Even when the situation cries death and hopelessness, fight the good fight of faith. Never give up, and never give in to the enemy's fear tactics. No matter what the situation looks like, with Jesus there is always hope. Hope for healing and miracles, and hope for a future. Remember, Jesus suffered and died in your place, and it was a horrible place, but then joy returned in the morning when He rose from the dead, and this is reason to stand fast for your miracle.

The enemy whispers wicked lies to implant seeds of doubt within your mind, because he knows it's the pathway to your heart. His vision is to steer you into the realm of unbelief, and his mission to get you to enter there is to steal your hope, kill your trust in Jesus, and ultimately destroy your life.

This is why more than ever before, you must hold up your shield of faith to ward off the fiery darts of the enemy; and every time he manifests with lies, symptoms, and complications, thrust your sword of the Spirit at him and declare God's promises to you instead. The devil is a liar, there is no truth in him. He is the father of all lies. Jesus is the Way, the Truth, and the Life. He is the God of all truth. In Jesus you will always find your hope, your reason to believe and to have faith.

It's your decision to pick up your spiritual armor and fight, or neglect the use of your armor and not to fight. But the Spirit of the Lord wants to encourage you to *"Fight the good fight of faith"* (1 Timothy 6:12).

With Jesus you always win.

In the next chapter we will challenge one another to encourage, pray, and activate faith not only for our personal lives, but for the lives of others.

Prayer

> *Dear Holy Spirit,*
>
> *I surrender all fear and doubt to You this day. I equip myself with Your might, and will not fight this battle in my own strength. When I feel weak, remind me of my reason to fight, the goal I will achieve, and the reason I win. Send Your reminders about my spiritual rights to be victorious in this battle. In Jesus' name, amen.*

Pledge

> I pledge to God and to myself to remain strong in the power of His might. I will keep the vision before me. I know my reason to fight. I will achieve my goal, because I know that Jesus is my reason to win. He has given me the spiritual rights to be victorious in this battle.

Questions for Chapter 4—Created to Win

1. What do we need to fight this battle successfully?

2. What's the first thing we need in our vision for the battle?

3. What's the second thing we need to add to create our vision for the battle?

4. What is the third part of this vision that we need to add?

5. What type of covenant do we have with the Father?

6. What is unique about this covenant?

7. What are we to do in a battle when we have done everything else?

8. What power does God expect us to rely upon during this battle?

9. How does the Belt of Truth protect us?

10. With the Breastplate of Righteousness, where does our righteousness come from?

11. Where do we prepare our feet with the preparation of the gospel of peace?

12. What part of our spiritual armor quenches the fiery darts of the enemy?

13. What does the Greek word *sōzō* mean?

14. Who is responsible to dress us with the full armor of God?

15. When the Red Sea is preventing us from entering into the Promised Land, why does God not part it for us?

Personal Reflection

I am encouraged by the fact that God created me to win. I have learned that I need to have a well-planned-out battle plan. What is my reason to fight this battle? What are my goals to accomplish in this fight against the spirit of death? What is my reason to believe I can win? And do I understand my spiritual rights to fight to win?

Group Discussion

Discuss the battle plan together, and help each other fill in the blanks so that each one in the group is confident to fight their battle to win. If you have time, discuss the four steps listed to take responsibility, grow up in the faith, activate it, and part the Red Sea that prevents us from entering into the Promised Land.

Chapter 5

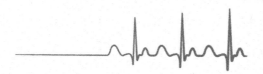

ENCOURAGE, PRAY, AND ACTIVATE FAITH

WORD OF THE LORD

The Lord God would say to you this day, "Reach out to those around you. Be not afraid to pray for them in My name. Offer to them the hand of healing. Many of them are without hope in the eyes of the world, but within you lies this hope—My hope, My healing power. Many of these people have been told there isn't anything anyone can do for them. But you have yet to offer them the prayer of faith for their healing. With Me and My Father, and by the power of My Spirit, all things are possible to them who believe. Believe who you are in Me, exercise the authority that I have given to you, and release this resurrection healing power and set the captives free. There is no reason for these people to be held captive by the deathly power of the enemy. Greater is My power within you—believe Me."

SHARE THE HOPE WITHIN YOU

The cynical attitude of the world has greatly infiltrated the Church. So much so, God's people often shy away from sharing the Good News about Jesus, and how He is able and willing to transform difficult situations. Frankly speaking, this should not be. People are so discouraged—they need the message of hope that you carry within you.

Why Hold Back?

Why do Christians tend to hold back from sharing their faith with others? First, because most are not being trained in the faith from the pulpit. Second, we hold back because we're not sure what to say. But I tell you from experience, if we spend time with the hurting, be sincere, and listen to them, they will tell us what they need to hear from us.

Make sure to pray before you visit them, and ask the Holy Spirit to lead you and guide you. He will show Himself faithful and strong to you, and you will know what to say. They don't want to hear some theological discourse from you, they just want to be encouraged with the hope of Jesus that you possess.

Encouragement

Always be willing to encourage others to trust God for a miracle. Your encouraging words and actions of support may be what the Lord will use to catapult these people into the realm of the supernatural power of the Holy Spirit where the answer to their needs manifests.

The following are five simple but important suggestions to remember when you meet with another to offer encouragement:

1. Be sincere.

2. Listen as if you truly care.

3. Don't be preachy or condescending.

4. Share words of hope.

5. Offer to pray in faith with them.

Pray for One Another

First Timothy 2:1 (NIV) encourages us to pray for all people: *"I urge, then, first of all, that petitions, prayers, intercession and thanksgiving be made for all people."* We need to get back to the basics in our faith and pray. Pray for one another in faith, pray believing that the much-needed results will come.

What is the difference between petitions and intercessions? A prayer of petition is to make a request for ourselves, whereas a prayer of intercession is to pray on the behalf of others. And this truly is a labor of love; you could spend this time and pray for your own needs, but instead you lift up the needs of another. And it follows right along the lines of Jesus' selfless example for us in that He is at the right hand of God and intercedes for us (see Romans 8:34). (Taken from the *Prophetic and Healing Power of Your Words,* Chapter 8, "Prayer Strategies," page 145, Prayer of Intercession.)

THE PROMISE OF FAITH-FILLED PRAYER

Do you doubt the power of your prayers? Do you sometimes wonder if your personal prayers will make a difference? This is what our enemy wants. He doesn't want you to pray with confidence. Why? Because it is the prayer of faith that makes all the difference.

> *Is anyone among you in trouble? Let them pray. Is anyone happy? Let them sing songs of praise. Is anyone among you sick? Let them call the elders of the church to pray over them and anoint them with oil in the name of the Lord. And the prayer offered in faith will make the sick person well; the Lord will raise them up. If they have sinned, they will be forgiven. Therefore confess your sins to each other and pray for each other so that you may be healed.*

The prayer of a righteous person is powerful and effective
(James 5:13-16 NIV).

No wonder the enemy wants us to feel insecure about our prayers. James tells us that our prayers of faith will save the sick, forgive sins, and bring healing, and our effective, fervent prayers will avail, profit, much.

> *Assuredly, I say to you, whatever you bind on earth will be bound in heaven, and whatever you loose on earth will be loosed in heaven. Again I say to you that if two of you agree on earth concerning anything that they ask, it will be done for them by My Father in heaven. For where two or three are gathered together in My name, I am there in the midst of them* (Matthew 18:18-20).

Jesus tells us in the Book of Matthew that whatever we bind, tie up, on earth in prayer will be tied up in Heaven; and likewise, what we let loose in prayer will be set free in Heaven. In other words, when we bind up with prayers of faith the spirit of death that is attacking us, it is bound to the command of our words. All of Heaven backs up this command. And by the same means of faith-filled prayers, when we release the healing power of the Holy Spirit into our bodies, the blood of Jesus secures the manifestation of it. But it all gets back to praying in faith.

Prayer and Declaration of Boldness

Dear Holy Spirit,
I pray in the mighty name of Jesus that I will be courageous when it comes to sharing my faith with others. I will not be intimidated to share the good news that I have been endowed with. I remind myself that I have been redeemed from the darkness of this world, not to hide my light under a bushel, but to let it shine forth from the depths of my very being. I declare that I will

be a light in the darkness; I will spread the truth that the God in Heaven truly loves and cares for the people around me. No longer will I linger in the shadows of fear, but I will come out from hiding and declare in these last days that I believe in Jesus. And I will act as though I really do believe. I will speak in love the truth about salvation to all those I come in contact with. I will readily lay healing hands upon the sick. I will boldly cast out demons. I will pray and speak forth in my heavenly language. I will not fear death, but put my trust in the power of Christ's blood to protect me from all evil. In the name of Jesus I put my trust, amen.

ACTIVATE FAITH

The Bible teaches us in the Great Commission that if we believe, we will lay hands on the sick and they will recover. When we believe in something, we activate our faith for it. Let's look at this in the natural. We hear the weather forecast, and the announcer says it is probably going to rain. So before we head out the door, we grab an umbrella. We read the almanac and it tells us that the frost will be gone in May, so to prepare to plant our gardens we purchase our seed in April. Toward the end of summer, we walk through our gardens and see the signs that it's time to harvest our crops. What do we do? We make ready our tools and round up our helpers and begin to pick our winter's supply of food.

And just as it is in the natural, so too is it in the supernatural realm. We hear that someone needs healing, or possibly the person in need of this healing is you. What do we do? The same as we would do in the natural, we grab hold of our faith in the redemptive work of Jesus. We read the forecast in our spiritual almanac, the Bible, that tells us that if we believe we will lay hands on the sick and they will recover. What do we need to do? Gather our tools, our healing hands, and our spoken words of faith, and put them to work for us so we can gather our supernatural harvest of healing and miracles.

CAN WE DO THIS FOR OURSELVES?

A man wrote to me, "Can I believe for this? Is it possible for me to fight for the life of my wife?" For a long time, God's people were led to believe that only the one standing in the pulpit could do the work of the Lord. And yes, those of us called to a ministry of healing have a special call on our life to do so. But God so wants people healed. He clearly says in the Great Commission, that if we believe, we will lay hands on the sick and they will recover (see Mark 16:18). He doesn't want anyone to miss out on the blessing and benefit of supernatural healing.

Yes, this man can believe for healing. And yes, it is possible for him to fight for the life of his wife. We should all freely release the healing power of the Holy Spirit to everyone around us.

WHAT TO PRAY?

When ministering the prayer of faith over someone, we need to be thorough with our words. Remember, our words possess the power of life and death and so we need to make sure we activate them wisely. For example, how should the man pray in faith over his wife? What should he say? I would suggest something like the following:

> *I curse cancer and all its cells and tumors at their very seeds, and command them to dry up at their roots and be eliminated from her body. I release the Spirit of Life, the Holy Spirit, to flow in and throughout her being, resurrect what is dead, awaken what is dormant, and recreate what is destroyed. I speak to every cell, tissue, organ, and system in this body to align itself with the Word of God, declaring that by His stripes (name) is healed and*

> *made whole, spiritually, emotionally, mentally, and physically*
> *all for the glory of Jesus, amen.*

And now, this man should continue to speak life, healing, creative miracles, and speak to his wife, giving her a reason to turn around in the valley of the shadow of death and return to this earth to fulfill her calling and destiny in the name of Jesus.

WE WERE BELIEVING—WHY DID THEY DIE?

A tough question I have heard asked, "Why do some people die when their family members and friends were believing for their healing, asking in faith, and speaking the Word over them?" What makes this question even tougher to answer is that we do not know all the variables or the people involved in the situation.

I have discovered that as I dig into these types of situations, people are not as firm in the faith as they say they are, or some members are very strong while others are weak. This mixture causes a problem. Doubt is just as powerful as faith, both involve activating words and actions, and our words and actions produce what they are released for. So there is an automatic conflict happening. Many say they believe, but as I listen to their words and watch their actions, I find their mind and emotions are riddled with unbelief. I don't believe this is intentional, but it is usually the case.

And I would have to say this comes from not being prepared in the Word as they should have been before the deadly attack upon their loved one happened. Therefore, they waver back and forth in their faith. One day they are strong in the faith, and the next day they are not.

I'm not saying this is an easy battle, because it is not. It takes strong faith to not waver when you hear serious medical reports, confront new emergency situations on a daily basis, see blood, machines and tubes, etc. These things plus human reasoning, the five senses, and negative emotions all work against the faith.

But I believe honesty needs to come into play at one point or another. The Bible teaches us, *"Therefore, confess your sins to one another, and pray for each other so that you may be healed"* (James 5:16 NIV).

It is human nature to not accept the blame for our shortcomings and wrongdoings, and a lack of faith for healing is coming up short, missing the mark, it's wrong. The only cure for doubt and unbelief is by reading and studying the Bible about a particular theme, in this case healing, until we can honestly say we believe. Otherwise we are just hoping God will reach down in His great mercy and heal the person, but deep down we have our doubts that He will.

I taught in detail in my last work, *The Prophetic and Healing Power of Your Words*, how to build a support team that works; see Chapter 17, pages 247-256. I encourage you to get a copy of it and read it. It will help you.

THIS IS NOT A GAME

I am often asked to pray for people while they are on their deathbeds. I remember a group of people were believing for someone to be healed, at least most of them were. Then the person just suddenly died. It was a painful loss for everyone involved. But right after the death, people started to say things to me like, "I knew all along he was going to die." These types of comments, especially this one, did not sit right with me. If this is the truth, then this person should never have been permitted into the inner circle of faith for the man's healing.

In essence this person had just said to me, "While others were believing for his healing, my faith was in his death." This is not a game. We are not playing "faith." We either believe or we don't. And if we find ourselves in the latter position, we need to make a decision to either do what needs to be done to get us to the point where we do believe, or humbly bow out of the situation and allow someone who does believe to take our place.

THE RECIPIENT'S RESPONSIBILITY

People on their deathbeds have a part to play in all of this as well. They need to possess the will to live. If they lack this basic element, there is not much you can do for them. In this case, love them and make sure they are right with the Lord concerning their salvation.

But just because they say in the beginning of the battle that they don't want to fight, doesn't mean you give up. Oftentimes, people are in need of some heavy doses of encouragement. They need a reason to fight, a goal they can achieve, and a reason to believe they can conquer the spirit of death. And this is where you come in and speak the truth to them in love. Shine the light of Jesus into their heart of despair.

If you are dealing with a young child, children tend to be very trusting and open to the healing power of Jesus, but you need to remember they are under the authority of their parents. It's the parents you need to reach with the message of faith.

What do we do if the recipient of all of our faith efforts suddenly gives up? This is a very common scenario. People are under a lot of stress, emotions are running high, the recipient is very ill and oftentimes is unable to cope with outside concerns and unresolved issues that are coming to the forefront. I find people are just not themselves, and it causes extra hurt and pain in an already painful circumstance.

Another common problem that occurs is that recipients of prayer feel like they are a burden to the family and feel uncomfortable, even guilty, about it. Medical expenditures are adding up and they are concerned about how the family will cope with it all. Oftentimes, the recipient is in so much pain from the illness that their faith is worn down and they lose the will to live.

So what do we do? I believe the best thing we can do is pour on the love and let them know that our love is unconditional. We are committed to one another in the good times as well as the bad times. And we are going to rally together and overcome this deadly disease once and for all.

I am a firm believer in life, and that we never give up on God, ourselves, or on each other.

ENTER INTO THE REALM OF FAITH BY HOPE

Perhaps you find yourself in the position of believing God for the impossible, but you are not sure how to get there. First of all, if you find yourself in the place of the impossible, then you are in right standing for a miracle. If it's possible in your own strength, then it's not a miracle.

Believing God for the impossible is entering into the realm of faith, and before you can have faith you must have hope—hope for the miraculous. Hope in the strength of God where you defy human wisdom and strength, and willfully deny your own human reasoning and the power of your five senses. The first step of faith may not be easy, but it is a must. You must have faith in God's supernatural ability to obtain a miracle.

> *Now faith is the substance of things hoped for, the evidence of things not seen* (Hebrews 11:1).

TO OVERCOME THE IMPOSSIBLE, YOU MUST DENY YOUR FLESH

The humble place of believing God for the impossible is often misunderstood by the world and even by many of our fellow believers in Christ. But in order to overcome the impossible situation, you must deny your flesh and your soul (mind and emotions) the pleasures of sympathy that doubt and unbelief produce, and believe God, no matter what. Look at all the good it produces—life, healing, restoration, joy, and a possible out of impossible situations. Believing God is well worth it all.

ACTIVATE FAITH FOR A MIRACLE

Jessica went into labor one month early and delivered a beautiful baby boy, but his lungs were not fully developed and he was struggling to survive. He was connected to a respirator for forty-plus days and fought infections from the breathing tube. They were told he would never survive. As time passed, the negative reports were solidifying in the minds and hearts of the family. But this family had a history of amazing miracles.

One major miracle was that of Jessica's brother, Henry, who was run over by a bus eleven years before. His legs were broken in numerous places, gangrene had set in, and the doctor was telling the family it was time to amputate. But they requested they be given three days for a miracle from their God. To their surprise, the doctor agreed, as long as they signed a release form releasing him from all responsibility.

Henry's parents activated the only thing they had—hope for a miracle. This couple went beyond the realm of hope and stepped into the atmosphere of faith where they would be able to manifest the healing and creative miracles they needed. And glory to God, Henry was delivered! His legs were healed from gangrene, saved from amputation, and new flesh grew.

But still Henry was not able to walk. They carried their teenage boy down the dirt road to our home, and we encouraged them in the faith, prayed over him, and activated our faith. He was instantly able to walk. In fact, he walked down a flight of stairs when the family left our home, walked across our soccer field, and down the dirt road to their home.

So you see, Jessica and Maurice and her family had a history of miracles. Why couldn't the miraculous be released again, this time on the behalf of their baby? One reason was the negative beliefs of the church they were under. Before the birth of this child she had a miscarriage, and during their time of great sorrow, they were told this was God's doing. This caused so much hurt and confusion, and made it difficult for them and their family to stand firm in the faith and believe in the goodness of God for the life of their baby.

With this information, you clearly see what I saw—a spirit of death was after the family. Numerous negative emotions that we spoke about in Chapter 2 had weakened their faith and opened the door for the spirit of death to remain and attack again. This demon is wicked and seeks to take advantage anyway it can, especially with those who cannot defend themselves, as is the case with this little baby boy.

And Maurice, the head of his household, did the right thing. He sought encouragement to believe. He first called and requested that I come and lay healing hands upon his baby. But for whatever reason, I was unavailable. My husband, David, stepped in and invited him over to come and talk. As they were talking, David realized that they had not given their baby a name or registered him because they feared he would not survive. David encouraged him in the faith, told him how to put his faith into action. The first act of faith was to name and register the baby the next day because he was not going to die, but live, and declare the works of the Lord (see Psalm 118:17). Then they prayed together. Maurice and Jessica ran with the hope for a miracle for their baby and activated their faith for him.

Their baby was instantly healed and released from the hospital. He is alive and thriving for the glory of the Lord!

TESTIMONY REVIEW OF FAITH STEPS

1. David took the time and listened.

2. Maurice shared his fear and doubt.

3. David addressed this issue of fear and doubt.

4. Gave simple steps to put their faith into action.

5. They prayed in faith together.

6. Maurice and Jessica put their faith in action.

7. And then the miracle manifested.

As we know, the spirit of death doesn't just attack us with sickness and disease, there are many other ways as well. How do we activate our faith in the midst of sudden and unexpected battles? Let's discuss this in the next chapter.

Prayer

> *Dear Holy Spirit,*
>
> *Help me to see the need in others. Remind me to put off self-ishness and take the time to reach out and minister to them. I desire to be about my heavenly Father's business in these last days and surrender my services to You from this day forward. In Jesus' name, I pray, amen.*

Pledge

I pledge to God and myself to repent from selfishness and to keep my spiritual eyes open to see the needs of others around me. I will be bold enough to offer them a word of encouragement. And I will pray and teach them how to activate faith against the spirit of death and to manifest their miracle.

Questions for Chapter 5—Encourage, Pray, and Activate Faith

1. Why do Christians tend to hold back from sharing their faith with others?

2. What do you need to do for the hurting to tell you what they need to hear from you?

3. What should you do before visiting the hurting?

4. What might happen with your encouraging words and actions to another?

5. List five simple suggestions to remember when you visit people to encourage them.

6. What is a prayer of petition?

7. What is a prayer of intercession?

8. According to James, what are the results of our prayers of faith?

9. What happens when we bind up the spirit of death with our prayers of faith?

10. According to the Great Commission, what will happen if we lay hands upon the sick?

11. What does the Great Commission tell us we must do in order to lay hands on the sick to recover?

12. Does God want anyone to miss out on the blessing and benefit of supernatural healing?

13. What is the cure for doubt and unbelief concerning healing?

14. What does the recipient need to possess in this battle?

Personal Reflection

When it comes to sharing my faith with others, do I hold back? If so, why do I do this? Am I a good listener? Or am I always preoccupied with other things when others are speaking? Am I willing to make the necessary changes to show others that I care and share the love and hope of Jesus that I have with others?

Group Discussion

Hold an open discussion with your group about why you hesitate to share your faith with others. Talk about the five simple suggestions to remember when you share your faith with others to encourage them. Share with one another good and bad experiences when you stepped out to share your faith and discuss how the situation might have been handled differently.

Part Three

OTHER WAYS THE SPIRIT OF DEATH ATTACKS

In Part Three we will talk about other ways in which the spirit of death attacks us. Be encouraged as I share three personal attacks against my family and how we overcame this demon of death in each situation by the supernatural interventions of God. Then we will take a hard look at self-inflicted death and wrongful behaviors that lead to death, and discuss what we can do to help ourselves and our loved ones overcome in the name of Jesus.

Chapter 6

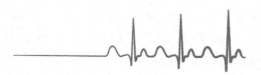

SUDDEN AND UNEXPECTED BATTLES

WORD OF THE LORD

I, the Lord your God would say to you this day, "Do not fear the sudden and unexpected attacks of the enemy. I go before you, I go behind you, and I also walk alongside of you. Have I not promised to be with you wherever you go? I have given to you everything that you will need as these last days are upon us. Your faith in Me and My Word will see you through these difficult days ahead."

As a prophetess and healing evangelist, I teach a lot about how the spirit of death attacks us with its major weapons of warfare—sickness and disease. But you know as well as I do this is not the only way this murderous demon of death attacks us. And we are going to take a good hard look at some of these different ways, and learn how to protect ourselves from premature death in the future of these last days.

It was the day before Thanksgiving in 1994. Our family decided to have a day at the beach together to celebrate the first of many

Thanksgiving Days to come in Guatemala. It was a perfect day in many ways. The sun was beating down on the black volcanic sands along the shoreline. We were enjoying the flavors of fresh, juicy watermelons and mangos, eating salty chips, and drinking icy cold bottles of Coke. The ocean was particularly calm that morning. We were all laughing and having a good time in the warm waters of the Pacific. We were experiencing all the elements of a great family day.

There was no hint of the sudden danger that was about to attack our family. As the five of us were running in and out of the ocean catching the waves and body surfing back to shore, a powerful and unexpected wave engulfed David and Annie and they were swept away by the powerful undertow in the ocean. I didn't know where they were. I couldn't see them. I ran up and down along the beach, but they were nowhere to be found. They were gone, drowning in the undertow. *"The waves of death swirled about me; the torrents of destruction overwhelmed me"* (2 Samuel 22:5 NIV).

As they were snatched away, David quickly grabbed hold of the back of Annie's swimsuit. As they were tumbling away in the violence of this undertow, her swimming suit kept wrapping around and around his wrist, almost to the breaking point, but he would not let go. In the confusion of the moment, they could not tell which way was up or down. *"The cords of the grave coiled around me; the snares of death confronted me"* (2 Samuel 22:6 NIV).

Every now and then they were able to gasp for a breath of air. Our 14-year-old daughter, Annie, cried out, "Oh God, we're going to die!" Her words sparked hope and the answer to the sudden and unexpected crisis they were caught in. David heard and responded, "Yes, God!" Immediately, when he called out those words, he literally felt a large hand from behind grab hold of them and push them out of danger and into the shallow waters onto the shore. *"He reached down from on high and took hold of me; he drew me out of deep waters"* (2 Samuel 22:17 NIV).

I shared in Chapter 3 about angelic help to those who inherit salvation, and we know that this hand was that of a ministering spirit. It was one of God's angels dispatched at the whisper of David's prayer, "Yes, God," and my prayer called out from the shore, "Lord, help us." We read about the security of the Lord for those who trust in God in Psalm 91:11-12, regarding God's rescue squad. In this instance, they were sent out on lifeguard duty. *"For He shall give His angels charge over you, to keep you in all your ways. In their hands they shall bear you up...."*

After a near-tragic incident, we often ponder in our minds the events that could have ended our lives. This situation was no different for our family. And in the center of these thoughts I asked God, "Why?" Why was the spirit of death after us that day? The answer came to me in the form of a warning filled with wisdom. Even though we were new to the mission field back then, we were a threat to the enemy and the darkness that he planned against other people. And I knew from that moment on I needed to go deeper in prayer for the protection of my family.

A DECREE OF FAITH

To protect you and your family from the evil workings of the spirit of death, build a wall of protection between you and it. Pray a decree of faith that separates you from its dangerous deeds. Cut off its power over you in the name of Jesus. Pray this decree of faith daily over your family for protection.

> *In the name of Jesus, I decree, cut off, and separate myself and my family from the evil tactics of the spirit of death. You will not fulfill your wicked ways with us. The Holy Spirit, our Guide, has shown to us your ways of destruction and death against us. But greater is our Savior Jesus in us, than you who are in this world. Be gone with you this day!*

Something we need to remember about a decree of faith, one time doesn't cover all time. We need to continue to decree words of faith daily. But the good news is, the power of faith-filled decrees work. So work them on your behalf and your loved ones.

A DECLARATION OF FAITH

Once you build that wall of protection with a *decree* of faith, then it's time to make a *declaration* of faith. A declaration of faith is declaring what you already have in your spiritual possession. In this case, you already possess God's protection by the atoning blood of Jesus. I have been daily declaring over myself and my family the following declaration of faith ever since I was a baby Christian, even several times throughout the day.

I want to share this with you because it is powerful and effective, and I have seen its results over and over again in the life of my family.

> *In the name of Jesus I declare that no weapon formed against us shall prosper. No evil can come near our dwelling, and every lying tongue set on fire against us will be silenced, exposed, and brought to shame, in Jesus' name, amen.*

ACCEPT THIS TRUTH

This is one truth that you should accept—as a believer of the Almighty God, you are a threat to satan and his demonic force. And he is looking for an opportunity to take you and those you care about out of this world. Why? Because in you is a greatness that outshines the darkness of this world. And this greatness is that of God, and a true glimpse of Him in you will rescue many from the evils of satan. The enemy fearfully knows this to be true. The question is, do you know this to be true? It's time to recognize God's greatness in you and be fully aware of what the spirit of death wants to steal from you—your time on this earth to be a mighty witness for Christ.

> *Do you not know that you are the temple of God and that the Spirit of God dwells in you?* (1 Corinthians 3:16)

> *That Christ may dwell in your hearts through faith; that you, being rooted and grounded in love* (Ephesians 3:17).

> *Jesus answered and said to him, "If anyone loves Me, he will keep My word; and My Father will love him, and We will come to him and make Our home with him* (John 14:23).

A LOVING FATHER

I appreciate the example of a loving father in this near-death experience. As David and Annie were tumbling out of control in the rip current, and Annie's swimsuit was twisting around and around David's wrist, he wouldn't let go of our little girl. This floods my soul with thoughts about our heavenly Father and how He holds on to us in the course of turbulent times.

> *For You, Lord, are good, and ready to forgive, and abundant in mercy to all those who call upon You* (Psalm 86:5).

> *God is our refuge and strength [mighty and impenetrable], a very present and well-proved help in trouble. ...Give thanks to the God of heaven, for His lovingkindness (graciousness, mercy, compassion) endures forever* (Psalm 46:1; 136:26 AMP).

> *The name of the Lord is a strong tower; the righteous runs to it and is safe and set on high [far above evil]* (Proverbs 18:10 AMP).

CALL OUT TO GOD IN FAITH

Have you been attacked by a sudden and unexpected battle? If so, call out to God in faith right now. It doesn't have to be a long and lengthy prayer, but it does need to be from your heart, sincere and full of faith that He is the One to help you in your time of need.

> *Let us therefore come boldly to the throne of grace, that we may obtain mercy and find grace to help in time of need* (Hebrews 4:16).

Your faith is so pleasing to God that it stops all of Heaven, so to speak. It grabs His attention and causes Him to stop and hear your plea. There isn't anything more pleasing to Him than to hear you speak to Him in His language—faith. And it's your contact point with God.

Faith doesn't bawl and squall about what it doesn't have or doesn't see. That's not faith; that's doubt and unbelief, which does not get His attention, nor is it well-pleasing to Him. Faith goes boldly before His throne of grace and it calls things that are not, as though they are already done. Faith trusts in God, not in circumstances or in the ways and wisdom of the world—only in God.

> *(as it is written, "I have made you a father of many nations") in the presence of Him whom he believed—God, who gives life to the dead and calls those things which do not exist as though they did* (Romans 4:17).

So whatever the need or the danger you are facing, whatever obstacle is standing in your way, you have a unique way to connect with God—your faith. And in the beginning your faith may seem insignificant, but the more you exercise it the stronger and more powerful it becomes. So go ahead, trust God, not your feelings or human reasoning or scientific findings; boldly trust God. The bolder the faith in Him, the quicker you capture His attention.

We talked about sudden and unexpected events that can lead to premature death and the reason behind these types of attacks. Let's now turn to the next chapter and see how God makes a way when there is no way to escape death.

Prayer

> *I pray, Father God, that You will fill the reader with great grace that only comes from You. And with this grace comes a completion of this person's time and destiny on earth that the enemy cannot steal it. This reader will fulfill his or her calling in these last days before Your soon return to take us up with You. In Jesus' name I pray, amen.*

Pledge

I pledge to God and myself to become more aware of the tactics of the enemy and dedicate more time to pray for protection for myself and my family.

Questions for Chapter 6—Sudden and Unexpected Battles

1. Why was the spirit of death after us that day on the beach in 1994?

2. What did I learn that I needed to do?

3. To build a wall of protection against you and your family and the spirit of death, what should you pray?

4. What's something we need to remember about a decree of faith?

5. What do we declare with a declaration of faith?

6. From your reading, what's one truth you should accept?

7. What does the spirit of death want to steal from you?

8. What should you do if you are being attacked by a sudden and unexpected battle now?

9. What should this prayer be?

10. What pleases God?

11. Where does faith go?

12. What is your unique way to connect with God?

13. What happens when you exercise your faith?

Personal Reflection

How do I feel about what I just read? Does this scare me? Or does it encourage my faith knowing that even in sudden and unexpected battles God is with me? Do I have a personal experience that I can prepare in my heart to share with others?

Group Discussion

Ask the group members to share a personal experience of when they were suddenly and unexpectedly attacked by the enemy, and how God's grace delivered them.

Chapter 7

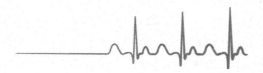

GOD MAKES A SUPERNATURAL WAY

WORD OF THE LORD

The Lord would say to you this day, "My people, you have entered into a time that many have longed to see. Trials will be great, but victories will be even greater. The spiritual darkness will become darker, much darker, but My light will shine brighter. Tough times will come for all, but My grace is sufficient to see you through all that you will face. And in the natural when there is no way, know that with Me all things are possible, and I will make a way of escape. I will remain faithful to you."

What do we do when we find ourselves in a deadly situation with no way of escape? Do we cross our fingers and hope for the best? Or do we put our trust in our God who is far superior than the danger we face? The latter choice is obviously the right decision, but do we have what it takes to trust Him like this? I believe we do; in fact, I know we do.

Why can my faith be so sure about this? Some would say it's because I have a life full of victorious experiences with Him. And yes, I can attest to this as being true, but it's not the whole truth. The experiences are just a result of something much deeper than amazing testimonies.

The reason my faith is so sure in Him is because I have come to know Him personally, and He has never failed me yet, and He never will: *"But the Lord is faithful, who will establish you and guard you from the evil one"* (2 Thessalonians 3:3). His faithfulness to each of us is something the enemy can't compete with.

Apostle Paul tells us in Second Timothy 2:13, *"If we are faithless, He remains faithful; He cannot deny Himself."* This is amazing—even if we are faithless, He remains faithful. How many times have we proven ourselves to be faithless in our beliefs about His redeeming power? Probably more times than we would like to admit. And yet, I totally believe this is where we miss out on His response to our needs time and time again.

It's this faithfulness of God that will make a way of escape to protect us from the wicked plans of satan. But how do we activate this faithfulness of His in our lives? The answer to this lies in First Corinthians 1:9, *"God is faithful, by whom you were called into the fellowship of His Son, Jesus Christ our Lord."*

CALLED TO FELLOWSHIP

It's one thing to believe and receive Jesus Christ as our Savior. And yes, it's the initial step to our salvation where we become a member of His family, a citizen of Heaven, and are called into His fellowship. But there is more to be had in this eternal relationship, and it's a step that many have failed to take. God desires us to enter into true fellowship with Him where we actually get to know Him personally. And it's in this personal fellowship with Him where these eternal benefits like provision and protection and the other benefits are actually activated.

Adam and Eve had perfect fellowship with God and because of it they had no lack—everything was instantly provided for them. But they carelessly forfeited it all, and Jesus had to come to this earth to restore what they had foolishly tossed away. Part of what Jesus came to restore was the personal fellowship between God and people.

The more we seek Him, the more we know Him. And the more we know Him, the easier it is for us to trust in His faithfulness to us. It's in this strong bond of trust that we can believe Him in all areas of life, including death and protection from premature death.

GOD MAKES A SUPERNATURAL WAY

Our son, Aaron, and I were following behind David and our two other children, Annie and Micah, through Mexico back to Guatemala from the United States. This was the trucker's route and this portion of the drive was hill country. This meant that the semis go up the hills slowly and faster on the downside of the hills.

It was a long day, and all had been going smoothly until we had to pass this one particular semi with a driver who I believe was drinking alcohol or doing drugs. I can't come up with any other logical reason for his bizarre behavior.

While we were passing this truck, the driver turned and looked at us and started to laugh as he deliberately sped up to not allow us to finish our pass safely. To make matters worse, there was a cliff to my left with a guard rail, but no shoulder to pull off onto. He was on my right side, and up and over the hill ahead of us came another semi-truck. There was no place for us to go. And the man just laughed away.

I had to remain focused, I could not think about death, only about living. My goal was to get us in front of this truck, and away from this madman. But he wouldn't let up. And now I have another semi-truck coming right at us. The driver of the other semi started to blow his horn and flash his lights. There wasn't anything I could do but try with all my might to get in front of this truck. And in the natural, it was not going to happen.

Neither my son nor I can explain what happened next, we just knew we were now safely in front of the semi and continuing on our way. It should not have turned out this way, we should have been dead, but we know that God caused something supernatural to happen. He made a way where there was no way in the natural for us to escape death.

I believe that if more of God's children would concentrate on life instead of death, many more will have the complete victory they seek.

TRANSLATED IN THE BIBLICAL SENSE

I have never shared this before because I didn't know how people would respond to it. I believe what happened to us that day was that we were supernaturally translated from eminent death to safety. There is no other explanation for it. I did not complete the pass around the truck. I remember gaining on the man's speed, but I never made it to the point to move over in front of him. I saw a bright light flash, and for many years I believed it to be the oncoming truck's headlights. But as I dare to look back on the situation, a set of headlights cannot make that large of a flash, and certainly not in the daylight.

As soon as I saw the great flash of light, we were safely in the other lane driving down the road, and a good distance in front of the madman in his semi. And as I looked up, I saw David and the kids in the van off in the distance on top of the other hill. They had stopped, and thought we were going to die. They didn't realize all that had taken place, and quite frankly, neither did we.

I also believe I have not shared this before because God has a timing for everything. And as we are living in these last days before we are called up to meet Him in the air, these supernatural interventions will become more common place for us all. Open your heart and get ready.

Biblical Example of Translation

We see an example of biblical translation in Acts 8:39-40: *"Now when they came up out of the water, the Spirit of the Lord caught Philip away, so that the eunuch saw him no more; and he went on his way rejoicing. But Philip was found at Azotus. And passing through, he preached in all the cities till he came to Caesarea."* What happened to Philip is described by the Greek word *harpazō* (Strong's G726), which means, catch (away, up), pluck, pull, take (by force). The Holy Spirit, plucked or pulled (translated) Philip from one place to another place on this earth supernaturally.

WHAT ABOUT ENOCH AND ELIJAH?

The Bible speaks of Enoch being taken away and Elijah being taken up in a chariot of fire. What actually happened to them? Let's do a little study with blueletterbible.org and find out.

In the Book of Genesis 5:23-24 the following account concerning Enoch is recorded: *"So all the days of Enoch were three hundred and sixty-five years. And Enoch walked with God; and he was not, for God took him."* And again in Hebrews 11:5 we find a second mention of this concerning Enoch: *"By faith Enoch was taken away so that he did not see death, 'and was not found, because God had taken him'; for before he was taken he had this testimony, that he pleased God."*

I appreciate how Hebrews 11:5 starts out, *"By faith."* I tell you, nothing of God can be accomplished, whether it be great or small, without faith in Him. And Enoch was certainly a man of faith. How do I know this to be true? Because the last portion of this Scripture tells me that *"he pleased God."* According to the Scriptures, there is only one way to please God and that is by faith.

> *But without faith it is impossible to please Him, for he who comes to God must believe that He is, and*

that He is a rewarder of those who diligently seek Him (Hebrews 11:6).

This word "please" in Hebrews 11:6 comes from the Greek word *euaresteō* and means to gratify entirely (Strong's G2100). And Enoch surely did just this, even his name means dedicated. What a beautiful testimony to have that you are dedicated and gratify God entirely.

The Bible says that Enoch was *"taken away."* This phrase "taken away" comes from the Greek word *metatithēmi*, and it means to translate, carry over, remove, change or turn (Strong's G3346). And he was taken away, translated, removed from this earth so that he would not see death. And the word "death" means exactly what we think it does. It comes from the Greek word *thanatos* and means the death of the body (Strong's G2288).

We should take note that in Hebrews 11:5 it mentions three times that Enoch was taken away. The Holy Spirit is making it clear that he was translated, removed from this earth without experiencing physical death. And the evidence that we have of this taking place is faith—it is the only evidence that we need.

"Now faith is the substance of things hoped for, the evidence of things not seen" (Hebrews 11:1). This word "evidence" means a proof, that by which a thing is proved or tested (Strong's G1650), *elegchos.*

Now let's study Elijah being taken up in a chariot of fire and find out what this means and what actually happened to him.

We read of this amazing account in Second Kings 2:11-12: *"Then it happened, as they continued on and talked, that suddenly a chariot of fire appeared with horses of fire, and separated the two of them; and Elijah went up by a whirlwind into heaven. And Elisha saw it, and he cried out, 'My father, my father, the chariot of Israel and its horsemen!' So he saw him no more. And he took hold of his own clothes and tore them into two pieces."*

This phrase "went up" is the Hebrew word *'alah* and means to go up, ascend, to climb (Strong's H5927). And this is what happened to Elijah the great prophet during the time of the reign of Ahab. A great chariot of fire descended and separated Elijah from his disciple, Elisha; and prophet Elijah ascended in a whirlwind into the sky until Elisha saw him no more.

JESUS AND US

This sounds similar to what happened to Jesus in Acts 1:9 when He ascended after His death and resurrection on this earth: *"Now when He had spoken these things, while they watched, He was taken up, and a cloud received Him out of their sight."* The phrase "taken up" is a Greek word *epairō* and it means to lift up, raise up, raise on high (Strong's G1869). In Acts it says that a cloud, a supernatural cloud received Him. This word "receive" is from the Greek word *hypolambanō* and means to take up and carry away (Strong's G5274). Even the phrase "out of" is from the Greek word *apo* signifying a separation (Strong's G575).

I want to look at one more instance of people being translated, and it involves all of us who are born again and is from First Thessalonians 4:17: *"Then we who are alive and remain shall be caught up together with them in the clouds to meet the Lord in the air. And thus we shall always be with the Lord."* Greek word *harpazō* (Strong's G726), which means, catch (away, up), pluck, pull, take (by force). One day all of us who believe in the Lord Jesus Christ will hear that great trumpet blow, and we will be instantly translated, caught up, plucked up from this earth to meet Him face to face in the clouds. This will not be an earthly cloud, but a supernatural cloud of His great glory for eternity.

STAYING ON TARGET

I made a comment in this near-death testimony that I want to expound upon a bit more. I said, "I had to remain focused, I could not think about death, only about living." If we concentrate on life instead of death, many more would have the complete victory they seek. In the midst of an attack from the enemy, no matter what type of attack it may be, I have found that the enemy wants us to focus on the wrong things. This way he can get us off track in the supernatural realm of the miraculous and onto his death track.

What do I mean? I could have spent those final moments yelling at the mad truck driver, but that would not have helped. And it would have frightened my son even more, as he and I were in this deathtrap together. That is what I think the devil wanted me to do—get me off God's track. God's track was for me to hold my peace and allow the Lord to fight my battle for me.

What battle was I engaged in? I was engaged in a face-to-face battle with the murderous spirit of death. And I tell you, we have to know how to fight this wicked demon—it's not with human power, but with the power of God that wins.

Do you think it was easy for me to hold my peace? I had my teenage son at my side, and the mother in me knew I had to protect him. There was no time for me to let my emotions get involved. No matter how bad it looked, and it was a bad situation, I had to stay on target and hold my peace.

> *Lord, you will give perfect peace to those who commit them-selves to be faithful to you. That's because they trust in you* (Isaiah 26:3 NIRV).

> *Peace I leave with you, My peace I give to you; not as the world gives do I give to you. Let not your heart be trou-bled, neither let it be afraid* (John 14:27).

For to be carnally minded is death, but to be spiritually minded is life and peace (Romans 8:6).

We've discussed some deep things of the Holy Spirit in this chapter, about how God makes a way—supernaturally—for us to escape death, and also how He transports His people from one place to another through this supernatural means of translating us. In the next chapter we are going to learn how we can have victory over deadly attacks.

A DECREE AND DECLARATION OF FAITH TO PRAY

Because of the dangerous times that we are living in, I think it is wise that we speak a decree of faith over ourselves and loved ones. Remember, with a decree of faith we build a wall of protection between us and danger. And so, let's build this wall.

By faith in the name of Jesus, I construct a wall of protection around my family. And the spirit of death cannot climb over it, dig under it, or break through this wall. It remains strong and steadfast. No matter the situation, the Holy Spirit always makes a way of escape from premature death for us by His supernatural power.

Just as a reminder, a declaration of faith is something we already have in our spiritual possession found in the Bible. An appropriate declaration of faith would be something like this: By the mighty, matchless power of the blood of Jesus, we have been rescued from the clutches of premature death. We declare we will not die, but live and declare the works of the Lord! (See Psalm 118:17.)

Pledge

I pledge to God and myself to put my trust in my Lord who is far more superior than the danger I face. I believe in His supernatural ways to make a way of escape when there is no way in the natural. I will not be closed-minded to His supernatural ways.

Questions for Chapter 7—God Makes a Way

1. What do we do when we face a deadly situation?

2. Do we have what it takes to trust Him?

3. What are translation experiences?

4. What can't the enemy compete with?

5. What does God do if we are faithless?

6. In our reading, what will God's faithfulness do for us?

7. What does God desire us to do?

8. What is part of the reason Jesus came to this earth?

9. In the testimony, what did I say I could not think about? And what did I think about?

10. What would happen if we concentrated on life instead of death?

11. What does the Greek word *harpazō* (Strong's G726) mean?

12. What did the Holy Spirit do for Philip?

13. How does how Hebrews 11:5 begin?

14. What is the Greek word for "please" in Hebrews 11:6 and what does it mean?

15. What does the Greek word *metatithēmi* mean?

16. What happened to Enoch?

17. What does the phrase "went up" mean? (Hebrew word *'alah*)

18.   What happened to Elijah?

19.   In Acts 1:9, what does the phrase "taken up" mean?

20.   What will happen one day to all those who are alive and believe?

Personal Reflection

How do I feel about what I just read? Is my level of faith where it should be? Or do I need to spend more time with the Lord in fellowship in His Word and on my knees in prayer so I can get to where I need to be in the faith? Do I really trust Him to make a way supernaturally where there is no way naturally? If not, am I willing to do whatever it takes to get to this level of trust?

Group Discussion

Ask if anyone in the group has ever had an experience, such as the one shared in the testimony, where they believe they were translated. If not, discuss their feelings about what was shared in this testimony. Be ready to minister to those who lost loved ones.

Chapter 8

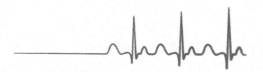

VICTORY OVER
DEADLY ATTACKS

WORD OF THE LORD

The Lord would say to you this day, "As these last days are being fulfilled, know that the enemy will fight against you with all his wickedness. Also know that I fight even harder to protect you from his vile attacks. But you too have a part to play—faith. Prepare yourself to walk in My victory against the enemy in these end days with the power of your faith."

We are living in a day and age when crime is out of hand and many people are being hurt and killed, including God's people. What does the Bible say about these times?

> *But mark this: There will be terrible times in the last days. People will be lovers of themselves, lovers of money, boastful, proud, abusive, disobedient to their parents, ungrateful, unholy, without love, unforgiving, slanderous, without self-control, brutal, not lovers of the good, treacherous, rash, conceited, lovers of pleasure rather than lovers*

of God—having a form of godliness but denying its power.
Have nothing to do with such people (2 Timothy 3:1-5
NIV).

From a dark and dank Roman prison cell the apostle Paul wrote
these words of warning to Timothy—and they apply to us today concerning the spiritual atmosphere of these last days. He warns us that the
last days will be filled with terrible, perilous times. Perilous means fierce
and full of danger.

People of this secular world are in a critical state; they have been
exposed to so much violence, many since they were infants, with
ungodly television shows, deranged movies, and violent video games.
Many children of this world have especially been affected by all this
filth and violence. Some play death, they clothe themselves with messages of death, and they listen over and over again to worldly music that
spews anything and everything, including violent and murderous acts
against others. Many have lost the reality between life and death. And
because they are filled to overflowing with the vile acts of satan, they
don't understand God and His ways, nor do they understand what it
means to live peacefully with people. It has never been modeled before
them. Everything is about me, myself, and I; they want instant gratification, at any price, as long as they do not pay for it.

This portion of Scripture in Second Timothy 3 prophecies that
people in these last days will be headstrong and haughty, and they are.
They are full of pride and unwilling to listen to reason. It's difficult,
if next to impossible to have a reasonable discussion with some. And
many are filled with a lying spirit, like their father the devil.

The Word says they will become despisers of good. And we are
seeing this prophetic writing come to fruition. Good is now bad, and
bad is now the new good. Those of us who stand up for righteousness
are insulted and attacked. And as we turn on the television or read the
news, it's as if the political leaders and the wannabe leaders are boldly

declaring their evil stances without shame. It's become a competition who can outdo who with their haughty boasts of wickedness to gain the popular vote of today's fallen society.

Some politicians lack boundaries and want no rules and regulations placed over them. They don't care about other people's property. If they want what you have, they openly take it. They don't care if they are being filmed or not. And if they don't like what you believe, they will unashamedly destroy what you have.

The Scripture passage from Second Timothy 3:1-5 says that the people will be *without self-control*. This word "self-control" comes from the Greek word *egkrateia* and it means the virtue of one who masters his desires and passions, especially his sensual appetites (Strong's G1466). But the society of the world is claiming there is no God in Heaven, and it's everyone for themselves. Without God, how can they have godly morals and gain restraints upon their greed and lust? So yes, times are terrible and perilous, and the Scriptures tell us that they are going to get worse.

We are witnessing society fall, and fall quickly. The wicked attacks against the unborn are blatantly evil and becoming more open and widely accepted by society. Children are killing children and their parents in alarming numbers; likewise, parents are killing one another and their children. People are violently attacking the elderly, one another, and themselves. The value of life is being stolen right before our eyes.

In Revelation 6:8, we read the apostle John's vision concerning the last days where he shares with us the following account of the fourth seal: *"So I looked, and behold, a pale horse. And the name of him who sat on it was Death, and Hades followed with him. And power was given to them over a fourth of the earth, to kill with sword, with hunger, with death, and by the beasts of the earth."*

Matthew 24:12 (NIV) tells us, *"Because of the increase of wickedness, the love of most will grow cold."* As we watch unrighteousness multiply on earth, we also witness the love of people wane. And the lack of love for God, for ourselves, and for others is very dangerous because faith operates by love. (See Galatians 5:6.)

So with this deathly type of prophetic utterance from the Bible, how do we protect ourselves and our loved ones from these deadly attacks? How can we have victory over our enemies? Let me share about a near-death attack I experienced, then we'll talk about how to protect ourselves and those we love.

NEAR-DEATH ATTACK

It was late afternoon and Joaquin went with a couple of his buddies on their motorcycles to the nearby town. Several hours had passed, it was dark and Joaquin knew it was time to return home, but his friends didn't want to leave just yet. So Joaquin came home by himself.

He was driving down the dirt road and making his way up the first hill when five young guys stepped out of the darkness to block the road with a long bamboo pole. He knew he was in trouble and tried to turn around to escape, but the gravel was soft and loose and with the incline of the hill the motorcycle slipped from underneath him. He was unable to get away from them.

They surrounded him, started to kick him, tied him up, screamed obscenities at him, and held a gun up to the back of his head. Joaquin was very afraid, and thought for sure they were going to kill him. They stole his personal belongings, threw him in the bushes, and hid his motorcycle out of view down in the ditch. Then they waited for their next victim.

Even though the situation was terrifying and his thoughts were racing every which way, at some point during all the chaos he was able to gather enough wits and cry to God for help. It was a simple, but heartfelt plea, "God, help me!"

My God is my rock, in whom I take refuge, my shield and the horn of my salvation. He is my stronghold, my refuge and my savior—from violent people you save me (2 Samuel 22:3 NIV).

Not too long afterward came another unsuspecting man on his motorcycle, and they started to do the same thing to him; but then came a car, and they stopped the driver. While they were harassing the driver of the car, the other guy on the motorcycle got away, but no one knew they had Joaquin tied up and hidden in the bushes.

Though I walk in the midst of trouble, you preserve my life. You stretch out your hand against the anger of my foes; with your right hand you save me (Psalm 138:7 NIV).

These five young hoodlums knew that the tables had been turned against them, and now they were in danger of being found out by the police, especially since the other man on the motorcycle escaped. And the man in the car could speak up against them if they were caught. The spirit of fear started to turn upon these young men, and confusion also was present. What were they going to do with Joaquin? The five guys were desperate, and desperate people rarely make good decisions. Joaquin knew they were coming back for him.

But this time they were not beating on him or screaming at him. They did not have a gun pressed into the back of his head either. Instead, they untied him, apologized to him, pulled his motorcycle out of the ditch, and helped him get on it, and sent him on his way.

What happened? I believe because we are a praying family, and we have taught all eight of our children to trust God and to pray, that God helped him. In the face of a deadly situation, Joaquin called out to God with sincerity of heart, "Help me!" And He did.

I called to the Lord, who is worthy of praise, and have been saved from my enemies (2 Samuel 22:4 NIV).

I believe the moment Joaquin called out to God, that warring angels were dispatched to rescue him. And just like they confounded the plans of the Egyptian soldiers in the middle of the Red Sea by pulling the wheels off the chariots, I believe they worked in the same manner for Joaquin.

When those angels caused the wheels on the chariots to fall off, they bought the Israelites time to reach the safety of the other side. Likewise, when Joaquin cried out to God for help, ministering angels sent confusion into the situation and the man in the car came along, and it bought time for the other man on the motorcycle to escape. This plan not only allowed the man to escape, but spared the life of Joaquin as well.

Now did Joaquin pray to angels for help? No, he cried out to his God—Jehovah. And it was the Lord who dispatched the angels on his behalf. Jesus, Yeshua, is our Savior in every situation we face.

In my distress I called upon the Lord, and cried out to my God; He heard my voice from His temple, and my cry came before Him, even to His ears (Psalm 18:6).

In my distress I cried to the Lord, and He heard me (Psalm 120:1).

In these two verses from Psalms 18 and 120, we read how David called upon the Lord, and cried out to Him, and God responded. The prayer of faith reaches the ears of the Lord, and He responds to it.

These words from the Book of Isaiah are amazing: *"It shall come to pass that before they call, I will answer; and while they are still speaking, I will hear"* (Isaiah 65:24). As God's people, we are not only to act, but to also speak out and pray in faith with confessions, declarations, and decrees of faith. We are to prophesy, call things that are not as though they already were (see Romans 4:17). And as we develop this lifestyle of communication of faith with God, amazing things begin to happen. You will see as you develop this type of prayer life that answers come before you need them.

For example, with Joaquin's situation, the man in the car didn't supernaturally appear, did he? No. But because we are a praying family who prays in faith for each other and the needs of our family, God's provision is there when we need it. I believe God directed this man, without his knowing, to leave at a specific time to be there just at the right moment when He would dispatch His warring angels to respond to Joaquin's cry to God for help.

A Scriptural prayer to pray over yourself and your family could be: *"Keep me safe, Lord, from the hands of the wicked; protect me from the violent, who devise ways to trip my feet. The arrogant have hidden a snare for me; they have spread out the cords of their net and have set traps for me along my path. I say to the Lord, 'You are my God. Hear, Lord, my cry for mercy'"* (Psalm 140:4-6 NIV).

PROTECTION FROM THE ENEMY

I strongly believe that protection from these types of deadly attacks come before they ever happen. What do I mean? I believe in the power of our spoken words. When we line up our words with God's and declare them over our family, we create a shield of protection around us that is very difficult for the enemy to break through.

In these last days, we need to spend more time in prayer interceding for the protection of our families. Pray in faith, declare the promises of God's Word over ourselves. The following are more Scriptures about God protecting His people from harm. Use them liberally when you intercede for your family:

Be strong and courageous. Do not be afraid or be terrified because of them, for the Lord your God goes with you; he will never leave you nor forsake you (Deuteronomy 31:6 NIV).

Then David said to the Philistine, "You come to me with a sword, a spear, and a javelin. But I come to you in the name of the Lord of hosts, the God of the armies of Israel, whom you have defied" (1 Samuel 17:45).

God is our refuge and strength, a very present help in trouble (Psalm 46:1).

Let's write a declaration of faith from these three verses I just added:

I declare that I am strong and courageous. I will not be afraid, for my God is with me wherever I go. He will not fail me or forsake me. Though my enemies come against me with a sword, a spear, a javelin, or present-day weapons, I will fight back with the name of the Lord. My God is my refuge and strength, a very present help in time of trouble.

Learn to use the words of God in your daily life, and watch the power behind them begin to manifest their message for you.

Be Aware

The enemy knows that his time is short, and so he is gathering his warring demons against us. A grave darkness has been released to steal, to kill, and to destroy us, but we do not need to live in fear. We do need to be aware of what is happening around us and exercise wisdom. Be prepared to call upon the name of the Lord in any situation you find yourself.

The Lord Goes with Us

> *When you go out to battle against your enemies, and see horses and chariots and people more numerous than you, do not be afraid of them; for the Lord your God is with you, who brought you up from the land of Egypt. So it shall be, when you are on the verge of battle, that the priest shall approach and speak to the people. And he shall say to them, "Hear, O Israel: Today you are on the verge of battle with your enemies. Do not let your heart faint, do not be afraid, and do not tremble or be terrified because of them; for the Lord your God is He who goes with you, to fight for you against your enemies, to save you"* (Deuteronomy 20:1-4).

These types of Scriptures are encouragements for us in the good fight of faith that we are required to fight. And even as our enemies rise up against us, and they will focus on these last days, let's choose to put our trust in our God rather than in the strength of their numbers or weapons. And remind ourselves in prayer that He is with us. He will fight to the finish for us. In the power of His might is where we find the victory in every battle, and with every enemy that will rise up against us.

In the next chapter we will discuss how a spirit of suicide has been released, how we can pray for people struggling with this, come up with a plan of action, and take a life challenge.

A DECREE AND DECLARATION OF FAITH TO PRAY

With the blood of Jesus, I raise up a standard of protection for my family and myself. I renounce wicked attacks from the enemy against my family. I declare you will not have your way with them. We have a blood covenant with God the Father that cannot be broken, and I activate these promises by my faith in His faithfulness to me, in the name of Jesus, amen.

Pledge

> I pledge to God and myself that even though we live in perilous times, I will not fear my enemy. I will trust my God to protect me and my family from the deadly attacks of satan and his spirit of death. I will prepare myself to call upon the name of the Lord in every situation I face.

Questions for Chapter 8—Victory Over Deadly Attacks

1. In Second Timothy 3:1-5, how does apostle Paul describe the times we are living in now?

2. According to Second Samuel 22:3, what type of people will God protect us from?

3. Even though we walk in the midst of trouble, what does Psalm 138:7 tell us God will do for us?

4. What have we taught all eight of our children to do?

5. In this testimony, what did Joaquin do?

6. What does Second Samuel 22:4 say happens say will happen when we call out to our God?

7. The moment Joaquin called out to God, what happened?

8. What happened when the warring angels caused the wheels to fall off the chariots in the Red Sea?

9. What happens when we line up our words with God's and declare them over our family?

10. What should we do in these last days?

Personal Reflection

Have I been filling my mind and the mind of my children with violence? Do I need to make changes in what we watch and listen to? Am I praying faith for protection over myself and my loved ones daily? Or do I need to step it up in this area and begin to pray for our safety? Have I taught my children to trust God and to pray?

Group Discussion

Discuss with your group members what concerns they have regarding the issues rising against us in these last days. Find out how they presently pray for their families. If they don't pray, encourage them to be praying for them. Talk about real topics that need prayer and pray for them together.

Chapter 9

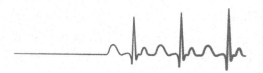

THE SPIRIT OF SUICIDE

WORD OF THE LORD

The Lord would say to you this day, "I have not left you, and I never will. I have gone before you in every trial. I have been tempted in every way, but I never gave in because I had you in My mind's eye. I love you with a love that the world does not understand, and it comes from the heart of the Father. I and My Father are one. We are united in Our quest for you. I realize that the enemy is bearing down hard upon you, but greater is My Spirit within you, than he who is in this world. Be not afraid and be not dismayed, for I am with you, always, even to the end of the earth and beyond."

An invasive army of demonic influence has moved in, and it's being led by one of satan's generals—the spirit of death. Suicide is taking place in grievous numbers.

We are living in a day and age when God is being removed from the hearts and minds of the people. And when tough times come, and they come to all, people who don't know Christ have nowhere to turn for help. Yes, God created human beings to encourage and stand with one another, but there are deep-rooted issues in life that God, Himself, is the only answer. And the devil is doing everything within his power in this late hour to hide from the people God and His plan of redemption.

Along with removing God from the hearts and minds of the people, the spirit of death and its evil ways are eroding away the value of life. We live in times when everything and anything goes, except God and His principles, which are being eliminated from schools, the government, even conversations. This leaves many people riddled with guilt and shame, with no knowledge of where to be cleansed spiritually. Emotionally they are void of the love of God. And without sensing the love He has for them, they can't love themselves. Nor can they love others around them.

In light of this epidemic, we as Christians need to be about our heavenly Father's business and teach people the truth, no matter what the world says they will do to us. Speak up and tell the truth. Tell people with both your words and by your actions, that God truly loves and cares for them. And so do you. Teach them who they really are in Christ, and that God is the Giver of Life, and He says that we always choose life.

Be real with the people; be willing and open to talk about the everyday issues that they are facing today. Don't be afraid to tell them what the Bible really has to say about present-day issues, no matter the topic—be honest. And in the Spirit of the love of Jesus, show them what God's Word says. Many people nowadays do not know about God and His Word and His ways. If Christians would do what they are commissioned to do—be the voice, hands, and feet of the Father—people would have hope and be better off than they are today.

CRY FOR HELP FROM TWO MOTHERS

I received the following two prayer requests on the same day within minutes, both from mothers hurting for their teenage daughters:

Please pray for my 16-year-old daughter to be healed of depression, anxiety, and cutting herself. Please pray that Jesus reveals Himself to her so she will believe again and follow Jesus Christ and come into her God-given purpose. Pray that our mother-daughter-father relationship will be healed between us as a family. Thank you and God bless you and your ministry.

Please pray for our adopted daughter who struggles with reactive attachment disorder, depression, and self-harm. She is currently in an inpatient treatment facility. She frequently experiences suicidal thoughts and cuts herself.

How do we pray in faith effectively for these girls and others fighting with suicidal thoughts and attempts?

First of all, we pray in the name of our Lord Jesus Christ on their behalf. His name is all powerful. His is the name above all names. He is the One to whom every knee will bow and every tongue will confess that He is Lord. This includes supernatural beings, angels and demons, as well as human beings. Praying in His name means we take our God-given authority over demons and take away their demonic artillery against our loved ones. In other words, we disarm them in the name of Jesus.

In the name of Jesus, I renounce this spirit of death, spirit of suicide, self-hatred, hatred of life, satanic influence, loss of identity and purpose, lying spirits, depression, fear and anxiety, and cutting herself. I release the healing balm of Gilead over her and that she is healed in her mind and emotions, all past hurts are healed with the oil of the Holy Spirit, that she will be able by faith, not by feelings, to forgive all that have wrongfully hurt her. That she will be able to let go of the past and move forward in life, living full of joy and hope for her future. I pray that relationships between parents and child will be healed, mended, and stronger than anyone ever thought possible. In Jesus' name, I plead the blood of Jesus over her, and I speak life over her for the glory of the Lord, amen.

PEOPLE NEED HOPE

People need hope to see them through the extremely rough times in life. Not only those who are struggling with suicidal thoughts, but also those closest to them. They need us to plant these seeds of hope in the garden of their hearts. Perhaps in the beginning they will reject what we have to say, but still certain things need to be shared, especially seeds of hope. Along with you, God will send others to water the hope seeds you planted. (See First Corinthians 3:6.)

Use the following Scriptures as you pray for them or with them, or add them to a little note of encouragement to let them know you are thinking about them.

- The prophet Jeremiah shares God's words of hope, and they still ring true in our hearts today: *"For I know the thoughts that I think toward you, says the Lord, thoughts of peace and not of evil, to give you a future and a hope"* (Jeremiah 29:11).

- Apostle Paul writes a beautiful prayer in the letter to the Philippians that resounds with hope even to this day: *"I thank my God upon every remembrance of you, always in every prayer of mine making request for you all with joy, for your fellowship in the gospel from the first day until now, being confident of this very thing, that He who has begun a good work in you will complete it until the day of Jesus Christ"* (Philippians 1:3-6).

- In the Book of Romans, the apostle Paul shares why hope does not disappoint: *"Now hope does not disappoint, because the love of God has been poured out in our hearts by the Holy Spirit who was given to us"* (Romans 5:5).

The next day I received another letter from a hurting young lady about the age of 19. She wrote from her heart, "Hello Becky, my name is Melissa. Without going into detail, I would like to ask you to pray for healing for me to be complete and whole. I have been through many unsettling and traumatizing situations in my life. I have committed many sins as well. I have attempted suicide numerous times, and have never succeeded. To God be the glory for that! I struggle with depression...."

How should we respond? We respond with sincerity of heart and with words of encouragement. Here is my response to this young lady.

Dear Melissa, I renounce the spirit of suicide and lying spirits over you. I release the healing balm of Gilead over your mind and emotions and that you are willing to go with Jesus into the deep corners of your heart. And by the healing power of forgiveness of those who have done you wrong, I declare you are healed and made whole. And all broken relationships that need to be healed, like with your parents, are healed for the glory of our Lord Jesus Christ. I am glad you are alive. I am proud of you for not going through with the devil's plan of suicide. God has a purpose and a destiny for you. And if you will completely give this painful area over to Jesus and allow Him to deliver and heal you from all of it, this can become your greatest strength—ministry to others who are struggling. Keep up the faith, forget the past, and move forward in Jesus' name, amen.

These are three letters I received in two days concerning three different girls struggling with life's hurts and believing the lies of satan that suicide is the answer. According to the organization Suicide Awareness Voices of Education (SAVE), females attempt suicide three times as often as males (CDC)[1]

General statistics for the USA from the same source:

- Suicide is the 10th leading cause of death in the US for all ages. (CDC)
- Every day, approximately 123 Americans die by suicide. (CDC)
- There is one death by suicide in the US every 12 minutes. (CDC)
- Suicide takes the lives of over 44,965 Americans every year. (CDC)
- The highest suicide rates in the US are among Whites, American Indians, and Alaska Natives.
- An estimated quarter million people each year become suicide survivors. (AAS)
- There is one suicide for every estimated 25 suicide attempts. (CDC)
- There is one suicide for every estimated 4 suicide attempts in the elderly. (CDC)

Global statistics (from the same source).

- Nearly 800,000 people die by suicide in the world each year, which is roughly one death every 40 seconds.
- Suicide is the 2nd leading cause of death in the world for those aged 15-24 years.

Obviously, females are not the only ones who attempt suicide; this same source reports that suicide among males is 4 times higher than among females. Male deaths represent 79 percent of all US suicides. (CDC)

A grandma wrote, "Prayer is needed for my 21-year-old grandson. The girl he believes he loves broke up with him and he has been dealing with depression and suicidal thoughts."

I responded, "Let's pray in Jesus' name. We renounce lying spirits and spirits of deception over him. I command you, satan and your demons, to leave him at once! Holy Spirit, please hover over him and cherish him. Don't let him go unattended by You and Your ministering angels. Father God, send Your angels to make war on his behalf, in the name of Jesus, amen and amen."

PLAN OF ACTION

While this grandmother and I are communicating back and forth, I suggest the following plan of action. This is something that she can personally do to activate the power of her faith for her grandson. I write, "As we are praying, I believe you need to fast for him for 3 days to break off this stronghold of suicide over him, and to break the soul ties between him and this girl. And during the wee hours of the morning, around 3:00 AM, get up and pray for him."

Three days later this loving grandmother wrote back, "I fasted for 3 days and got up at 3:00 A.M. like you suggested. The next day he had asked his dad to take him to the hospital. I believe my prayer made a difference."

I respond, "O yes, your prayer and fasting bumped him into reasonable thinking and I believe saved his life. Keep up the confession of faith."

WHY PRAY DURING EARLY MORNING HOURS?

Why should we pray for our loved ones struggling with suicide during the wee hours of the morning? I had this discussion with a group of leaders a few months earlier. It was between meetings and several of us were speaking about the tough issues of life that both the Church and the world are facing, and the subject of suicide came up. One of the participants in the discussion shared how a Christian radio station in Puerto Rico receives very serious phone calls from their listeners during the very early hours of the morning, when most others are asleep, and how they have prayed for many who were contemplating suicide during those hours.

I wanted to know if there was some validity to what this man was sharing, other than experience, so I investigated the issue on the Internet to share with you:

- Researchers determined that the suicide rate per hour rose to 10.27 percent after midnight. It peaked at 16.27 percent between 2 and 3 a.m., and then dropped to 2.13 percent between 6 a.m. and midnight, according to *CBS Atlanta.*[2]

- "When evaluated across the 24-hour day, and accounting for the proportion of the population likely to be awake, completed suicides are far more likely to occur at night (between midnight and 4:00 A.M.)," Michael Perlis, PhD, associate professor, Department of Psychiatry, and director of the Penn Behavioral Sleep Medicine Program at the University of Pennsylvania in Philadelphia, told Medscape Medical News.[3]

With this confirmed information from credible sources, I suggest to all Christians, if you know someone who is suicidal, lay down your comfort and fast for them for three days, whatever type of fast the Lord shows to you, and pray between the hours of 2:00 A.M. to 4:00 A.M.

Renounce spirits of death and suicide that are tormenting them, and release the Spirit of Life over them. Pray that the Holy Spirit hovers over them with His divine hand of protection. Release in the name of Jesus God's ministering angels to war on behalf of their life. Pray for an inner healing of their mind and emotions to take place, and that they would be able to forgive those who have hurt and disappointed them. And always pray in the name of Jesus for them.

YOUR FAITH CAN SAVE A LIFE

Your gift of faith—no matter the measure, even if it is the size of a mustard seed—when actively shared with others with your faith-filled words and prayers can make the difference, and can actually save a life.

I received the following letter from a dear woman who was fighting with a spirit of suicide, but something miraculous happened, and it started with words and prayers of faith. May this personal letter that I share with you touch your heart, and open your spiritual eyes to understand the importance of your faith-filled words. The woman wrote:

> Earlier this week I wrote out a suicide letter and spent a while contemplating it. Afterward I tore the pages from the notepad and destroyed them. As I did, your name was written on the page beneath the ones I tore out as I had watched you on Sid Roth [television host of *It's Supernatural*] and had written along with it the confessions for healing that you spoke.
>
> I had been having a rough time sleeping due to the mental anguish, and I'm in a lot of physical pain also. And when I eventually fell asleep that night, I woke from a dream in which I was being healed. I'll never forget how I woke as my dog sat beside me on the bed as if she were trying to keep me

safe. I was still in a lot of pain and decided to go and research your name and buy a book. I couldn't decide which one so I found your YouTube channels and watched almost all of the videos on there. I felt the very tangible power of the Holy Spirit in your words and I slept for almost 12 full hours the next night, and in much less pain.

As I started reading *DARE to Believe* on my Kindle, the torment began to ease and I found the exercises so easy to follow. I know I have a lot more healing to do, but I feel I have the right instruction manual, and feel more positive that I can do this. When I read the part about accepting Jesus as my Lord and Savior, I didn't just read it with my mind, I felt every cell in my body accepting Him, giving life to my bones.

I just wanted to thank you for sharing your gift with us. I believe my faith is being restored along with my physical body, and with it my mind is being renewed, and hopefully my family and life and relationships too. By faith in Jesus' name, thank you.

My response:

In the name of Jesus I release the Spirit of Peace over you, over your mind and emotions that they are healed and made whole. Jesus loves you with an unconditional love. He is always for you, and never against you. There isn't anything you can do to earn His love, and there isn't anything you can do to lose His love for you. He loves you whether you love Him or not. We have the promise in His Word that His precious thoughts toward you outnumber the sands of this earth. I am so thankful to Jesus that you are alive.

Someone I Love Committed Suicide

The following is an example of the pain someone goes through who has lost a loved one via suicide: "Lord, I am hurting really bad on the inside because (name) committed suicide. I am really struggling to make sense of it all. Help me to sort out my feelings. Sometimes I am angry with them for giving up on life. But mostly I just hurt, and the pain and the loneliness of this grief is more than I think I can bear. Holy Spirit, help me come to a place of peace with this great loss. Heal this emptiness in my heart. I miss them so much. I need Your grace more than ever now. In Jesus' name, I lay my sorrow down at Your feet, amen."

I Don't Know What to Say

One person wrote in regard to a loved one who tried to commit suicide: "I don't know what to say." I think most people struggle with what to say at a time like that. And perhaps in a crisis such as this, the most important things we can say are, "I love you, and I'm glad you are alive."

And this leads us to the following life challenge.

A LIFE CHALLENGE

What do you suppose would happen if we as the body of Christ started to release words of encouragement and hope to those around us and started to tell people close to you and even random people you come in contact with, *"I'm glad you're alive!"* You might think that would be uncomfortable to say to someone, but what if that person was actually fighting with negative thoughts of suicide?

- What if you said that to a teenager being fed lies from the enemy that suicide is a trendy thing to do?
- What if it is a man who just lost his job, everything he owns, and lost his purpose for living?

- What if the woman at the checkout counter was just served divorce papers the day before and is seriously struggling with thoughts to end it all by taking her life?
- Or it's a youngster being bullied at school and believes the taunting lies about being unloved and unwanted?
- Or it's someone whose body is so racked with physical pain that he or she feels it's impossible to continue on?

We don't know what is going on in the hearts of other people, but God does. And He might be sending you to deliver a message of hope to them. I fully believe that our words of encouragement can actually make a difference—and save lives!

This has been a tough chapter, but a necessary one. And we are always better equipped after we discuss the issues. Let's turn to the next chapter and see how we help ourselves and those we care about to overcome alcohol and drug addictions, biblically.

Prayer

Dear Holy Spirit,

Help me to discern when those around me are contemplating suicide. Help me not to fear to speak up and give an encouraging word of hope to these people. May my hope-filled words be the wake-up call they need, and spare a life for Your glory, amen.

Pledge

I pledge to God and to myself to be aware of the people around me. Not to be selfishly in a hurry, but to be willing to spare a moment and give them a friendly and heartfelt word of encouragement and hope, and tell them, *"Hey, I'm glad you're alive!"*

Questions for Chapter 9—The Spirit of Suicide

1. As Christians what do we need to do in this late hour?

2. In whose name do we pray?

3. With our God-given authority, what do we take away from demons?

4. What do people need to see them through extremely rough times in life?

5. How should we respond to people struggling with suicidal thoughts?

6. Is there evidence that people commit suicide more frequently between the hours of 2:00 and 4:00 a.m.?

7. What are two things that I suggest you do for someone you love who is struggling with thoughts of suicide?

8. What are the most important things you can say to someone who tried to commit suicide?

Personal Reflection

Am I struggling with suicidal thoughts? If I am, then I need to call one of the hotlines provided and get some real help. Or am I hurting because someone I love is dealing with suicidal thoughts? Am I suffering with the grief of a loved one who committed suicide? If so, I need to reach out to someone I can speak to about the hurt and the loss I'm feeling.

Group Discussion

Talk openly about suicide; encourage each other about the importance we have to one another. Let everyone in the group know that you are there for them at any hour to pray if they find themselves struggling with this evil temptation. Realize that many people have suffered the loss of a family member, friend, neighbor, classmate, or a coworker who has taken their life, and may be hurting from the loss. Pray for one another or for those they know are struggling with this. Make available the following contacts:

- National Suicide Prevention Lifeline[4]

Suicide[5]

- Suicide Hotline: 1-800-273-TALK (8255)
- Suicide Prevention Hotline: 800-827-7571
- Deaf Hotline: 800-799-4TTY
- NineLine: 800-999-9999
- Holy Spirit Teenline: 800-722-5385
- Crisis Intervention: 888-596-4447
- Crisis Intervention: 800-673-2496

ENDNOTES

1. SAVE, Suicide Awareness Voices of Education; https://save .org/about -suicide/suicide-facts/; accessed May 29, 2019.

2. "Study pinpoints when people are most likely to commit suicide"; *CBS News*, June 3, 2014; https://www.cbsnews.com/news/study-pinpoints -when-people-are-most-likely -to-commit-suicide; accessed May 29, 2019.

3. Megan Brooks, "Suicide More Likely After Midnight," Medscape, https://www.medscape.com/viewarticle/826054; accessed January 23, 2019.

4. National Suicide Prevention Lifeline; https://suicidepreventionlifeline .org; accessed May 29, 2019; 1-800-273-8255.

5. Pastor Bryan Lowe, "24/7 Crisis Lines," *Broken Believers,* January 23, 2011; https://brokenbelievers.com/2011/ 01/23/247-crisis-lines; accessed May 29, 2019.

Chapter 10

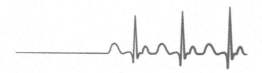

ALCOHOL AND DRUG ADDICTION

WORD OF THE LORD

The Lord would say to you this day, "I will that you would turn to Me on bended knee. I desire to hold you and heal you and set you free. But this can only happen if you will come to Me and lay your heavy burden down at My feet. If you will give it to Me, I will take it from you. And as you allow Me to cleanse those deep dark secrets from your heart, you will see your deliverance start, and the freedom that you so desire begin to manifest. I love you with an everlasting love—your Jesus."

Oftentimes people war against themselves, they struggle with past hurts and disappointments, and they turn to the bottle, to pills, or whatever they can find to forget about the pain for a while. Sometimes it's out of guilt and shame because of something they did or they didn't do and people were hurt. The enemy constantly taunts them with the memory of it, and to temporarily escape, they drink and do drugs.

Young people often hang out with the wrong crowd and do all the wrong things, then they become addicted and can't seem to break free from the bondage of alcohol and drugs.

When children grow up with parents who are addicted to drugs or alcohol during their formative years, and even though they swore they never would do as their parents did, they often repeat what was lived out in front of them.

Many people have fought in wars and have never been the same since the tragic events they witnessed and participated in. Trying to escape the reality of the past, they try to drink it away, but the pain never goes away in this manner. And years later they can't seem to break the bondage of addiction.

Others are bound to pain caused by serious illness or near-death accidents and can't handle the physical pain and have turned to drugs and alcohol to try to free themselves from the physical suffering.

Whatever the reason, it's all another plan of that serpent of old—satan—to keep people in bondage to the spirit of death. Instead of turning to God, they turn to synthetic help—alcohol and drugs. They and their families deal with an additional problem—addiction.

ADDICTION TO PRESCRIPTION DRUGS

A desperate woman writes, "Please pray for God to deliver me from addiction, severe withdrawals, depression, and anxiety. I was given medication and was not told it was addictive. Now my life is falling apart. Please pray for me for complete healing and deliverance in the name of Jesus Christ!"

Another woman writes, "Please pray for my brother. He had cancer and became addicted to opioids."

My response: "In the name of Jesus I renounce this spirit of addiction, severe withdrawals, depression, and anxiety. I renounce this spirit of bondage and command it to release you in the mighty name of Jesus.

I command this spirit of death out of you at once! I release the healing balm of Jesus to flow in and throughout your mind and emotions and that they are healed and made whole for the glory of Jesus, amen."

ILLEGAL DRUGS

"Please pray for my son who took drugs, meth, pills, and anything that would get him high. About 6 years ago he started hallucinating, and went to the hospital. Now 6 years later he is very anxious, talks to no one, he is full of fear and stays in his room. Please pray that his mind returns to normal again."

My response: "In Jesus' name I renounce the inner pain and fear from all the years of drug abuse. I pray that whatever doors were opened during the abuse of drugs are supernaturally closed. But before they close, I command whatever entered into them while open to vacate this young man. Holy Spirit, hover over him, bring him the peace, love, and acceptance that he truly needs and only comes from You. I speak healing into his mind and emotions for the glory of the Lord, amen."

ALCOHOLISM

A hurting woman writes, "Please pray for my husband who has been very ill and struggles with alcoholism. My kids and I are suffering terribly from his drinking."

My prayer for this man and his family, "In the name of Jesus, I pray for a revival to break forth over your family, and that it starts with the head of the house, your husband. I pray, Holy Spirit, hover over this man and convict him of his wrong behavior. I pray for an inner healing to take place within his heart, that with Your help he is able to forgive all that have wrongfully hurt him and walk away from life's disappointment. Forgive him, he does not understand the harm that he is causing his wife and children. And I pray for his wife and children that they too will be healed from the inside to the outside, walking in the Spirit of love and forgiveness toward one another. I pray for an intervention of the Holy Spirit to manifest in the midst of this family. I curse this spirit of alcoholism over him and this family, in Jesus' name, amen."

IS ADDICTION A DISEASE?

Is addiction a disease? This is a good question. The world claims that it is, but what about God? What does His Word have to say about this? Let's search out the Scriptures to find out.

Let's begin with the basics. The dictionary definition of addiction is the state of being enslaved to a habit or practice or to something that is psychologically or physically habit-forming, as narcotics, to such an extent that its cessation causes severe trauma.[1]

The world of psychology believes that addiction is a disease. Here is a direct quote from the American Society of Addiction Medicine:

> Addiction is a primary, chronic disease of brain reward, motivation, memory and related circuitry. Dysfunction in these circuits leads to characteristic biological, psychological, social and spiritual manifestations. This is reflected in an individual pathologically pursuing reward and/or relief by substance use and other behaviors.

> Addiction is characterized by inability to consistently abstain, impairment in behavioral control, craving, diminished recognition of significant problems with one's behaviors and interpersonal relationships, and a dysfunctional emotional response. Like other chronic diseases, addiction often involves cycles of relapse and remission. Without treatment or engagement in recovery activities, addiction is progressive and can result in disability or premature death.[2]

I agree with most of this explanation except for the following words, "chronic disease of brain reward, and like other chronic diseases." The world is prideful and has removed God from life, except when there is a tragedy, then they remember God and place the blame on Him—which in essence is refusing to accept responsibility for our wrong doings and placing the blame on someone or something other than ourselves.

This same scenario took place back in Genesis when Adam and Eve's lust for the forbidden fruit was manifested and found out. Neither accepted the blame for their own disobedience to God's rules, but instead passed the blame to another. This is interesting and still happens today.

> *And they heard the sound of the Lord God walking in the garden in the cool of the day, and Adam and his wife hid themselves from the presence of the Lord God among the trees of the garden. Then the Lord God called to Adam and said to him, "Where are you?" So he said, "I heard Your voice in the garden, and I was afraid because I was naked; and I hid myself." And He said, "Who told you that you were naked? Have you eaten from the tree of which I commanded you that you should not eat?" Then the man said, "**The woman whom You gave** to be with me, **she gave me of the tree, and I ate**." And the Lord God said to the woman, "What is this you have done?" The woman said, "**The serpent deceived me, and I ate**"* (Genesis 3:8-13).

The chain of blame holds people in bondage as we see here. Adam blames Eve for giving him the forbidden fruit, but in reality blames God for giving him the woman in the first place. And so often we will hear people jokingly blame it all on Eve, but as we see in the Scriptures, Adam was there when she ate the fruit.

> *So when the woman saw that the tree was good for food,*
> *that it was pleasant to the eyes, and a tree desirable to*
> *make one wise, she took of its fruit and ate.* **She also gave**
> **to her husband with her,** *and he ate* (Genesis 3:6).

Adam could have rebuked Eve and told her no, but he did not. He was an accomplice to this crime.

And then we look at this passage again and think, *Wow! That's very arrogant of Adam to speak so disrespectfully to God and tell Him that He's responsible for this mess.*

Allow me to challenge you with this common response, "I will not accept the fact that the devil put this sickness upon me. I refuse to say that I was overtaken by the devil. It was God who permitted this, and this is the reason why I am sick." Just like Adam, people blame God for their troubles all the time.

Let's go back to Adam's first crime—where did it begin? Sin begins in the mind, in the realm of our thoughts. The Word instructs us what to do:

> *For the weapons of our warfare are not carnal but mighty*
> *in God for pulling down strongholds, casting down argu-*
> *ments and every high thing that exalts itself against the*
> *knowledge of God,* **bringing every thought into cap-**
> **tivity to the obedience of Christ,** *and being ready to*
> *punish all disobedience when your obedience is fulfilled*
> (2 Corinthians 10:4-6).

Satan planted the seed of temptation to disobey in Adam's mind with negative words, and he dwelt on this thought and acted upon it and sinned against God.

The Bible tells us in James 1:14 (NIV), *"Each person is tempted when they are dragged away by their own evil desire and enticed."* Ponder upon the way this verse is written in the Amplified Version of the Bible,

"But each one is tempted when he is dragged away, enticed and baited [to commit sin] by his own [worldly] desire (lust, passion)."

Now, let's backtrack just a bit. It wasn't just Adam who did not accept the blame for his sinful actions, Eve did the same. When God asked her why she had committed this sin, she blamed the serpent who tempted her: *"The serpent deceived me, and I ate"* (Genesis 3:13). How often do we hear people say, "The devil made me do it!" No, satan did not make you sin. Yes, he tempted you, but you made the decision to sin all on your own. You are responsible for your sin.

First Corinthians 10:13 clears this matter up of about who is responsible: *"No temptation has overtaken you except such as is common to man; but God is faithful, who will not allow you to be tempted beyond what you are able, but with the temptation will also make the way of escape, that you may be able to bear it."*

People argue, "That's easy for God to say, He's God. He's a supernatural being. He doesn't know what it's like for us here on earth." But this argument is totally wrong. He knows *exactly* what we go through from His own personal experience. Hebrews 4:15 explains how Jesus was tempted when He walked this earth in human form: *"For we do not have a High Priest who cannot sympathize with our weaknesses, but was in all points tempted as we are, yet without sin."*

Do we think the temptations Jesus had to overcome were somehow easier than what we need to overcome? Back in Jesus' day there was rebellion, lying, cheating, stealing, murder, prostitution, and other sexual sins, drunkenness...and this list goes on and on, just as it does today.

Not only did He show us by personal example that it *is* possible to overcome temptation, He loved us so much that He took it a step further in the Garden of Gethsemane. He was about to enter into His final hours on this earth and be slaughtered because of our sin, to redeem us from it and its consequences, such as sickness and disease and other forms of the curse. Let's read this portion of Scripture from the Book of Luke 22:41-44 from the Amplified Version of the Bible.

> *And He withdrew from them about a stone's throw, and knelt down and prayed, saying, "Father, if You are willing, remove this cup [of divine wrath] from Me; yet not My will, but [always] Yours be done." Now an angel appeared to Him from heaven, strengthening Him. And being in agony [deeply distressed and anguished; almost to the point of death], He prayed more intently; and His sweat became like drops of blood, falling down on the ground.*

As we study this out, we see that Jesus was being tempted by the enemy, satan, not to fulfill the plan of atonement for us. And I personally believe this was the greatest temptation of all time, but even though He was being tempted, He did not sin. And what I teach people with this portion of Scripture is that it was at this point in time that Jesus overcame the human will so that we could overcome it as well.

We are talking about biblically overcoming addiction—and no matter what the addiction is, whether an addiction to drugs, alcohol, sex, pornography, gambling, or food, we have the ability with God to overcome any and all forms of addiction. But we must look at addiction through the eyes of truth. According to the Word in John 8:32 (NIV), *"You will know the truth, and the truth will set you free."* Blaming others and bad situations in life does not help, and calling addiction a disease does not set people free either. In the natural, disease needs medicine or medical treatments; we do not overcome addiction by becoming addicted to something else. Calling addiction a disease gives us an excuse to continue choosing this sinful, addictive behavior.

So is addiction a disease? No, it's a sin.

DELIVERANCE FROM A SPIRIT OF ADDICTION

The power of addiction is real, it's like a giant-size wrecking ball destroying individuals, marriages, families, businesses, ministries, communities, cities, and even nations. It's wreaking widespread devastation in the lives of people throughout the entire earth, including the body of Christ. We can see the suffering it causes within the soul—the mind and the emotions—and in the physical realm. But what the world, and oftentimes the Church, refuses to address is the root of the problem, the spirit. And until the spiritual aspect of this widespread epidemic is attended to, people will continue to be enslaved to the addiction and its destructive behaviors and results.

Addiction is more than a physical problem, it's an evil spirit—a demon that has taken control of the mind and the emotions and works its evil into the physical realm of the individual and all those with whom they come into contact. But even though, humanly speaking, the situation looks impossible, it is not. There is hope—His name is Jesus Christ, and with Him all things are possible, including freedom from addiction.

To be free from addiction, we need to be delivered in the name of Jesus and by the power of His blood. Why do we need to be delivered in the name of Jesus? Because according to God's Word, *"That at the name of Jesus every knee should bow, of those in heaven, and of those on earth, and of those under the earth, and that every tongue should confess that Jesus Christ is Lord, to the glory of God the Father"* (Philippians 2:10-11). And when we have the revelation that addiction is a demon, our faith can arise to the occasion and take our God-given authority in the name that is above every name and demand this evil spirit out of ourselves and/or our loved ones.

Also, to be free from addiction, we need to be delivered by the power of the blood of Jesus. Why? According to Isaiah 53:4-5 Jesus was whipped and shed His blood so we could be healed in spirit, soul, and body. When we spend the time and rightly divide the Word, we can determine that Isaiah 53:4-5 addresses holistic healing. That the atonement, the redemptive blood of Jesus, does in fact provide spiritual, emotional, and physical healing. (For a greater understanding see Chapter 2, pages 33-41, in *The Healing Creed*.) This includes deliverance from demonic forces that come to steal, to kill, and to destroy us; see John 10:10.

> *But [in fact] He has borne our griefs, and He has carried our sorrows and pains; yet we [ignorantly] assumed that He was stricken, struck down by God and degraded and humiliated [by Him]. But He was wounded for our transgressions, He was crushed for our wickedness [our sin, our injustice, our wrongdoing]; the punishment [required] for our well-being fell on Him, and by His stripes* (wounds) *we are healed* (Isaiah 53:4-5 AMP).

Deliverance from addictions come in all forms. It depends upon the strength and familiarity of the demon. In other words, how long has the person been walking hand in hand with this demon? And how far into the darkness of sinful behavior has this person willingly gone with this evil spirit?

Sometimes all it takes is a prayer of repentance and the person is free from demonic behavior, because it's just that—ungodly behavior. But other times the demon does not want to let go of the person because it inhabits, possesses the individual, and it's not going to leave its abode without a spiritual fight.

Now you notice I wrote a "spiritual fight." You cannot force a demon out of someone with physical force or by physical means, it's a *spiritual* battle. For example, screaming at the demon or physically slapping the individual does nothing to the demon. In fact, the demon is enjoying your display of ignorance and it wants you to make that person suffer more. It knows at that point you do not know who you are in Christ, and you are unaware of the authority in the name and in the blood of Jesus that you have been given.

To force this demon to leave, you have to create a spiritual atmosphere that the demon cannot handle being in. This means you have to activate spiritual weapons that are supernaturally stronger than it is.

Demons obey the following:

1. The authority of the name of Jesus. (See Philippians 2:10.)

2. The supernatural activation of the power of the blood of Christ. (See Isaiah 53:4-5.)

3. You—when they know that you clearly understand that you have dominion over them. (See Luke 10:19.)

To create the right atmosphere:

1. Spend time in prayer and fasting to break the power of the spirit of death and the spirit of addiction: *"So Jesus said to them, 'Because of your unbelief; for assuredly, I say to you, if you have faith as a mustard seed, you will say to this mountain, "Move from here to there," and it will move; and nothing will be impossible for you. However, this kind does not go out except by prayer and fasting'"* (Matthew 17:20-21).

2. Activate the fruits of the Spirit—they fuel your faith, make it operational: *"But the fruit of the Spirit is love, joy, peace, longsuffering, kindness, goodness, faithfulness, gentleness, self-control. Against such there is no law"* (Galatians 5:22-23).

3. Pray in the Holy Spirit.

- You need to activate supernatural power over the enemy: *"But you shall receive power when the Holy Spirit has come upon you; and you shall be witnesses to Me in Jerusalem, and in all Judea and Samaria, and to the end of the earth"* (Acts 1:8).

- The Holy Spirit will pray through you what is needed: *"Likewise the Spirit also helps in our weaknesses. For we do not know what we should pray for as we ought, but the Spirit Himself makes intercession for us with groanings which cannot be uttered. Now He who searches the hearts knows what the mind of the Spirit is, because He makes intercession for the saints according to the will of God"* (Romans 8:26-27).

- You need to keep yourself strong throughout the entire battle: *"Anyone who speaks in a tongue edifies themselves, but the one who prophesies edifies the church"* (1 Corinthians 14:4 NIV).

4. And you will need to usher the doubters and unbelievers from the premises where the deliverance will take place. You may actually need to leave the place that is familiar to the one possessed by the demon and bring the person into your territory where, hopefully, it is saturated with the presence of the Lord: *"When Jesus came into the ruler's house, and saw the flute players and the noisy crowd wailing, He said to them, 'Make room, for the girl is not dead, but sleeping.' And they ridiculed Him. But when the crowd was put outside, He went in and took her by the hand, and the girl arose. And the report of this went out into all that land"* (Matthew 9:23-26).

WHAT TO DO AFTER DELIVERANCE

After the deliverance has taken place, you must do the following as we are taught in Matthew 12 to keep the demons from returning:

> *When an impure spirit comes out of a person, it goes through arid places seeking rest and does not find it. Then it says, "I will return to the house I left." When it arrives, it finds the house unoccupied, swept clean and put in order. Then it goes and takes with it seven other spirits more wicked than itself, and they go in and live there. And the final condition of that person is worse than the first. That is how it will be with this wicked generation* (Matthew 12:43-45 NIV).

- **Transform your mind.** Renew your mind and your ways as you read God's Word: *"My son, give attention to my words; incline your ear to my sayings. Do not let them depart from your eyes; keep them in the midst of your heart; for they are life to those who find them, and health to all their flesh. Keep your heart with all diligence, for out of it spring the issues of life"* (Proverbs 4:20-23).

- **Develop a relationship with God.** Pray, talk to God in your natural language and build yourself up as you pray in the Holy Spirit: *"Then you will call on Me and come and pray to Me, and I will listen to you"* (Jeremiah 29:12). And again in First Corinthians 14:4 (NIV), *"Anyone who speaks in a tongue edifies themselves...."*

- **Listen to praise and worship music.** Keep the spiritual atmosphere clean as you listen to praise and worship music: *"See then that you walk circumspectly, not as fools but as wise, redeeming the time, because the* *days are evil. Therefore do not be unwise, but understand what the will of the Lord is. And do not be drunk with wine, in which is dissipation; but be filled with the Spirit, speaking to one another in psalms and hymns and spiritual songs, singing and making melody in your heart to the Lord, giving thanks always for all things to God the Father in the name of our Lord Jesus Christ, submitting to one another in the fear of God"* (Ephesians 5:15-21).

If you will work these Scriptures out to the fullest, you can find the freedom from addiction that you and your loved one so desire.

As a side note, I would never align myself with people who do not believe and practice the power of the Holy Spirit. If they do not actively live out this supernatural power, then they are weak in the faith and dependent on their own strength. You have already seen in your own life how weak your own strength can be. You need the power of the Holy Spirit to overcome this addiction in your life.

BIBLICAL WAYS TO OVERCOME ADDICTION

So many Christians are in bondage to addictive behaviors; they want to be free, but don't know how. One such young woman came forward for ministry at a healing conference in Kentucky. Her addiction was cigarettes and it had control over her—but she wanted deliverance and freedom. I laid hands upon her and renounced the spirit of addiction in her, and declared that from now on when she would try to smoke a cigarette she would start to vomit. She put it to the test. As soon as the service was over, she ran outside and took a puff of a cigarette and her body immediately started to vomit on the church steps. Her body now rejected what it once craved. But along with physical deliverance, her soul, mind, and emotions needed to be healed and renewed to remain free from the addiction.

You may be like this woman with an addiction to some type of sinful behavior and need deliverance and renewal of your mind. So, the following is a plan of action from the Scriptures to help you overcome any and all addictive behaviors:

1. Before you can overcome an addiction you first have to admit that you have a problem and that it is a sin. James 5:16 (NIV) instructs us to: *"Confess your sins to each other and pray for each other so that you may be healed. The prayer of a righteous person is powerful and effective."*

2. Make a quality decision that you will do whatever is necessary to be free from this ungodly behavior. There is a plan to freedom in James 4:7, *"Therefore submit to God. Resist the devil and he will flee from you."*

How do you submit to God and resist the devil?

- Ask God for forgiveness. *"If we confess our sins, He is faithful and just to forgive us our sins and to cleanse us from all unrighteousness"* (1 John 1:9).

- Read the Bible and cleanse yourself spiritually. *"That He might sanctify and cleanse her with the washing of water by the word"* (Ephesians 5:26).

- Listen to faith building messages. *"So then faith comes by hearing, and hearing by the word of God"* (Romans 10:17).

- Fast and pray for deliverance. *"So He said to them, 'This kind can come out by nothing but prayer and fasting'"* (Mark 9:29).

- Pray in the Spirit to encourage yourself. *"But you, beloved, building yourselves up on your most holy faith, praying in the Holy Spirit"* (Jude 1:20).

- Take control of your thoughts. *"Casting down arguments and every high thing that exalts itself against the knowledge of God, bringing every thought into captivity to the obedience of Christ"* (2 Corinthians 10:5).

- Confess out loud the promises of God over yourself. *"Death and life are in the power of the tongue, and those who love it will eat its fruit"* (Proverbs 18:21).

- Keep your joy level strong. *"...Do not sorrow, for the joy of the Lord is your strength"* (Nehemiah 8:10).

- Be full of the Holy Spirit. *"And do not be drunk with wine, in which is dissipation; but be filled with the Spirit, speaking to one another in psalms and hymns and spiritual songs, singing and making melody in your heart to the Lord, giving thanks always for all things to God the Father in the name of our Lord Jesus Christ"* (Ephesians 5:18-20).

- Don't take on stress or worry. *"Be anxious for nothing, but in everything by prayer and supplication, with thanksgiving, let your requests be made known to God"* (Philippians 4:6).

- Be accountable and surround yourself with supportive people. *"Do not be deceived: 'Evil company corrupts good habits'"* (1 Corinthians 15:33).

A spirit of addiction is out to control and destroy you. To be free, you have to make a quality decision that you will do whatever it takes to be delivered from its destructive power. If you will do these things on a daily basis, eventually you will break free from sinful and addictive behaviors. The enemy will flee from you, and the freedom you so desire will be yours.

ONCE AN ADDICT, ALWAYS AN ADDICT?

Is it true, "Once an addict always an addict"? No, you don't have to remain an addict, unless you want to stay an addict. I know many people who have been delivered from alcohol and drug addiction, and other addictions as well. The addictive powers have completely lost their power over these redeemed individuals. The redemptive power of the blood of Jesus is greater than addiction. Hold on to God's promise that every knee will bow and every tongue will confess that Jesus is Lord, including a spirit of addiction.

I taught you in my last work, *The Prophetic and Healing Power of Your Words,* about the power of your words, including labels such as "alcoholic." And spoke of alternatives to the world's lifelong labels. Declare a new label over yourself—healed, delivered, and made whole in the name of Jesus.

FORGIVENESS

I have witnessed time and time again the power of forgiveness to heal people spiritually, emotionally, mentally, and physically. If you are bitter toward someone in your family or a friend for their addiction and the harm it has caused you, it's time to forgive. If you don't forgive them, you bind their problem to you; and not only do you harm them, but you also hurt yourself.

God's Word plainly tells us, *"For if you forgive other people when they sin against you, your heavenly Father will also forgive you. But if you do not forgive others their sins, your Father will not forgive your sins"* (Matthew 6:14-15 NIV).

Let's pray this prayer together:

Father God,

I know Your Word says to forgive them, but I struggle to do so. Holy Spirit, I need Your strength to do this by faith in accordance to Matthew 6:14-15. In Jesus' name I forgive (name) for their addiction and all the problems and the stress they have caused in my life. And by faith I forgive them, and I release them from my bitterness and my vengeance. And in forgiving them I am forgiven of my many sins, and in releasing them from my bitterness and vengeance I am set free from the stronghold of their bondage too. Father God, I ask for Your love for them that covers a multitude of sins. In Jesus' name I pray this in faith, amen.

We've taken a good hard look at alcohol and drug addiction and have seen in the Bible how people can be delivered physically and healed in their mind and emotions from a spirit of addiction. Now it's time to turn the page and...

Prayer for Myself

Dear Holy Spirit,

I admit that I have a sin issue with addiction. I desire not to be controlled by this substance or activity any longer. I want to be free, and I understand that I am the one who determines my freedom. Help me to confess my sin to others who can hold me accountable for my behavior and support me in this freedom process. In Jesus' name, amen.

Prayer for My Loved One

Dear Holy Spirit,

I lift up (name) to You. I intercede on his/her behalf that they will surrender this sin of addiction to You. They will choose to do whatever it takes to be free from this bondage once and for all. I pray for inner healing to take place within their mind and emotions. That any brain damage and damage to other organs from all the years of drug and alcohol abuse are healed and made whole. I hold them up with the prayer of faith for their deliverance from this addiction, and I believe in the power of Your name, that they are transformed for Your glory, amen and amen.

Pledge

I pledge to God and to myself to be honorable and upright in all my ways. To be brave enough to get the help that I know I need. To stop blaming others for my poor choices. I move forward in the power of Your grace. And even though it may be difficult, I declare that I can do all things through Christ who strengthens me.

Questions for Chapter 10—Alcohol and Drug Addiction

1. Is addiction a disease?

2. Besides being a physical problem, what is addiction?

3. Before you can overcome an addiction, you have to first admit what?

4. To overcome an addiction, you have to make a quality decision to do what?

5. Is it true, "Once an addict, always an addict"?

6. Why is this saying not true?

7. Instead of declaring yourself an alcoholic or drug addict, what new label should you declare over yourself?

8. What happens if you will not forgive others of their addictions and the harm they caused you?

9. What happens if you do forgive them for their addictions and the harm they caused you?

Personal Reflection

Am I struggling with an addiction? Do I need to reach out for help? If not me, do I have a loved one who has an addiction problem that is hurting me and the rest of the family? Do I need to forgive this person? Am I willing to let them know that I love them and forgive them, and show them that I care? Is it time to reach out and try to set up an intervention for them?

Group Discussion

Talk openly among yourselves about alcohol and drug abuse. Discuss what it takes to submit to God to overcome an addiction. Then pray for one another as the Holy Spirit leads.

ENDNOTES

1. Dictionary.com, s.v. "Addiction," http://www.dictionary.com/browse/addiction?s=t; accessed May 30, 2019.

2. "Definition of Addition," American Society of Addiction Medicine, http://www.asam.org/resources/definition-of-addiction.

THE WARRIOR CONQUERS THE SPIRIT OF DEATH

In Part Four we will start out by following the voice of hope and learn how to discern lying spirits that will try to lead us into a trap of doubt and unbelief. You will also learn how to overcome by the blood of the Lamb, and how to declare and praise your way out of death. Together we will face the fear of death in these last days and release the warrior within us.

Chapter 11

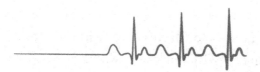

FOLLOWING THE
VOICE OF HOPE

WORD OF THE LORD

The Lord your God would say to you this day, "Be still and know that I am God. Quiet the raging storm within you, and allow My Spirit to speak to you. Let Me minister into the depths of your wound. Receive My healing balm, let it seep into the weepiness of it and cleanse the infection from the world from the inside to the outside. Hear Me this day, listen to what My Spirit wills to speak to you today."

Do we realize that we have the life of God within us? We have His DNA, His very nature, His miracle-working ability deep inside of us. We are created by His seed, and it's only natural for us to live and overcome the powers of death.

Spiritually speaking, it's unnatural for us to be filled with sickness and disease and to desire to stop living, or to end the life of another—that's the carnal nature, the old self resurrecting and dominating who we really are. We are actually spirit beings filled with the breath of God, housed in human bodies while on this earth.

We are not created for mere existence, but are destined for His greatness to multiply and fill this earth with His goodness and grace, life and healing, creativity and beauty wherever we go.

It is not the will of God that His life in us is overshadowed by the spirit of death. We are created to be overcomers in every area of life, not to concede to the darkness of our enemy—the devil and his wickedness.

It's time for each of us to become who we really are created to be—overcomers, life-givers, a generation of hope that spreads the Good News of salvation to a darkened and dimmed world that is crying out, "Give us hope!"

BELIEVE AND RECEIVE HIS PROMISE OF HOPE

In order for us to live the abundant life God has designed for us, we have to be able to believe and receive His promises of hope. How do we arrive at the level of faith where we don't doubt Him and His ways? It begins with love—His great love for us.

We live in an earthly realm where everything is based on conditions, especially love. If we do a certain thing, this will happen. If we don't perform the duty just right, it won't happen. If we conform to the world's way, we are accepted by them. If we dare to be different, they reject us. Quite frankly the world cannot love as they should, because they lack the Source of love—God.

But God isn't this way. His love for us is not based upon certain criteria that must be met. He loves us regardless of what we have or have not done. Even when we are at our worst, He still loves us as if we are at our best.

He doesn't see as the world sees; they see through a tainted glass of impurity, but God sees us through His eyes—with the clarity of love.

So yes, to believe and receive His promise of hope we need to believe that He loves us—and He does.

GOD IS WILLING AND ABLE TO BLESS YOU WITH GOOD GIFTS

God is good and is both able and willing to bless you with good gifts. It says in the Amplified Bible in Ephesians 3:20, *"Now to Him who is able to [carry out His purpose and] do superabundantly more than all that we dare ask or think [infinitely beyond our greatest prayers, hopes, or dreams], according to His power that is at work within us."*

The words, "superabundantly more" refer to God's generosity toward us. It says, *"all that we dare ask or think [infinitely beyond our greatest prayers, hopes, or dreams], according to His power that is at work within us."* What is this power that is working within us that activates His generosity toward us? It is the power of true hope and faith.

Faith is trust. Although, it's trusting for more than just basic needs; it's confident that He is willing to give you the desires of your heart. First John 5:14-15 says, *"Now this is the confidence that we have in Him, that if we ask anything according to His will, He hears us. And if we know that He hears us, whatever we ask, we know that we have the petitions that we have asked of Him."*

TOO MUCH TO ASK FOR

A woman wrote to me, "Becky, my situation is complicated. I am elderly, and my doctor says there isn't anything he can do for me. And given the circumstances, I'm wondering if my healing is too much to ask for?"

Regardless of how impossible the situation looks, the Lord is both able and willing to do exceedingly abundantly above all that we ask or think. You are meditating upon the possibility of your body being healed and released from the power of the spirit of death. You are envisioning yourself living pain-free and delivered from this wretched disease.

Brother or sister in Jesus, this is the Holy Spirit working in your heart, giving you hope for your future. And yes, our Lord is not only able to heal you, but He is willing to heal you, too. I encourage you this day not to give up, but to fight the good fight of faith, and put all your hope and trust in the redemptive work of Jesus Christ to heal you in spirit, soul, and body. Allow His healing power to work a miracle within you that will testify to future generations of His great glory forever.

Your healing and deliverance from the suffering caused by the spirit of death is not too much to ask for. His desire is that we believe and receive from Him His message of hope that He so freely gave to all.

ASK WITH BOLDNESS

Are you timid when it comes to asking God for something you need or want? Does the Lord want you to be shy with Him? Or should you come to Him with boldness?

A couple of years ago I asked one of the newer girls in our children's home what she would like for Christmas. She quietly whispered, "A little bag of chips." I said, "No, I'm not going to give you a snack-size bag of chips for Christmas." She didn't know how to respond, so I asked her if she would like a toy or a doll. She lit up on the inside, which turned to a big smile on the outside when she heard me suggest a doll, and said, "Yes, I want a doll!" Needless to say, you know what she received for Christmas.

But this got me to thinking about how and why we respond to our Lord sometimes. Just like this little girl, we were walking hand in hand, just talking together. God wants to do the same with us. Yes, He wants to take you by the hand and walk with you, talk with you, and just be with you.

I can just envision Jesus saying to us, "Say, you know what? I love you, and I want to do something real special. I want to bless you. What would you like to have?"

Many of God's people act like the shy little girl and do not know how to come boldly before His throne of grace and make their petitions known. Hebrews 4:16 sends out the following invitation to us, *"Let us therefore come boldly to the throne of grace, that we may obtain mercy and find grace to help in time of need."* And Philippians 4:6 also says, *"Be anxious for nothing, but in everything by prayer and supplication, with thanksgiving, let your requests be made known to God."*

Don't be afraid to ask God for what you need, or for the desires of your heart. He wants to bless you above and beyond what you can even possibly think or imagine.

Let's face it, God is a Giver. John 3:16 says that *God so loved the world that He gave....* He loves to give us good gifts (see James 1:17) like salvation, the Holy Spirit, healing, deliverance, wisdom, and provision to name just a few of the most important ones. And He's asking you, *"What can I give you today that will bless you?"*

Maybe you're even more like this little girl—maybe no one has ever demonstrated how much they really care. Perhaps you're uncomfortable with the fact that He loves you. God wants to take you by the hand and show you how to trust Him and how to be confident in His goodness toward you. He desires to embolden you with the power of faith so that you will not hesitate to run directly to His throne of grace anytime you have a need.

Jesus doesn't want you to miss out on any of His benefits that He so generously lavishes upon us. He's the Giver of life, both eternal and abundant life on this earth. And He's asking you, "What can I give you today that will bless you, I mean really bless you?"

PRAYERS OF DESPERATION

When people lack hope and the understanding that God loves them, they can easily fall into a pit of despair become desperate and easily swayed by lying spirits.

A woman wrote to me today requesting prayer for her and her husband to conceive a child. She is getting older and the doctor told her that it's next to impossible for her to become pregnant. But she says she is so desperate to have a baby that she is fighting with suicidal thoughts. This is a desperate woman; she longs to bear her own child, but a lying spirit is messing with her mind and emotions, telling her to end her life, while she believes to conceive a life within her.

A man wrote to me the other day concerning his daughter's need for prayer, "It tortures me to no end knowing that my God can heal her... yet...has not."

Wrong doctrine like this leads people to despair and causes them to pray prayers of desperation and speak out words filled with hopelessness. These wrong doctrinal beliefs do not lead anyone to wellness. God is not withholding healing from anyone. We have to learn how to believe and receive from God once again.

A man wrote for healing prayer from stage 4 prostate cancer and says that he can't continue on anymore. He needs to ask himself what he's really saying. Is it that he doesn't know *how* to continue on, or that he's lost hope and is unwilling to do so? And who is he listening to?

DISCERNING LYING SPIRITS OF HOPELESSNESS

In order to follow after the voice of hope, we have to be able to discern a lying spirit of hopelessness and be able to distinguish who is speaking to us. So often before the manifestation of a desired miracle manifests, the enemy will throw a wicked wrench in the wheel and derail people off their victorious track and into the enemy's plan of disaster and pre-mature death. They become so discouraged, they give up.

One Christian couple in ministry shared with me that they have had to fight off lying spirits of hopelessness from other people in the ministry. Their words do not line up with God's truth that she is healed by the blood of Jesus. They keep coming at them with discouraging words that just do not match God's healing promises.

I give thanks to the Lord that this Christian couple knows the heal-ing word, but not everyone does. Nor do they have the conviction to tell people to please refrain from praying faithless prayers over them.

I remember the time I was with a group of Christians around the bed of a dying woman. I was so appalled by the lack of faith that was being prayed over this sister in the Lord. The man of the house allowed anyone to come in and pray whatever they wished over his wife. He allowed three pastoral friends to come in, and one of the pastors knelt down at her bedside and started to cry out to God such inappropri-ate words of doubt and unbelief. I could not believe what my ears were hearing from this pastor, and his two buddies didn't pray any better.

I find it grievous how ill-prepared servants of the Lord can be when it comes to matters of faith. And they encourage their congregants to doubt the promises found throughout the Bible concerning their health and healing. Their Sunday messages are filled with despair about a false religious doctrine about a God who doesn't care.

I can't tell you the countless messages I receive every day from Christians searching for someone to encourage them in the faith to believe God for a miracle.

One woman I know of, before she passed from this earth to her eter-nal destination, left her lifelong place of worship for another because even though they did not know her, they offered her a message of hope.

Another woman in her final days said that a butterfly flew into her room and an inner voice told her that God was not going to heal her, and that she needed to give up and die. Another woman said an angel appeared and gave her this same message to stop fighting, and that God was not going to heal her. They both became so discouraged and emotionally hurt that they gave up, and a few days later died.

A woman recounted what happened to her mother. A hospice worker came to their home and tried to convince her mom to give up and die. It made her daughter uncomfortable, and it also upset her mother so much that she didn't want her to come to her home again.

What are we listening to? Are we listening to a message of hope? Or are we being deceived by the enemy and believing a message of hopelessness from a lying spirit? Does the message we hear line up with God's Word, or is it contrary to His promise of hope?

Does God's Word Tell Us to Give Up and Die?

Is there any place in God's Word that tells us to give up and die? No, we do not read this type of deadly message in the Bible. And if God's Word does not say this, then neither should we tell other people or ourselves to give up and die. In fact, we read the opposite in Deuteronomy 30:19 where God tells us to choose life. And this is the message we should share with others. Choose life, eternal life with Jesus, and abundant life with Jesus on this earth.

JESUS DOESN'T LISTEN TO DISCOURAGING VOICES

Jesus received urgent news to come and pray for His friend, Lazarus. But He is delayed in His arrival. And when He arrives, Lazarus' sisters tell Him that He is too late—their brother is now dead. To the natural mind the situation is beyond all possibility of healing. But this doesn't seem to bother Jesus.

Jesus goes to the tomb, they roll the stone away, and He cries out, *"Lazarus, come forth!"* And his body that has been dead for four days obeys His command of faith, and Lazarus' spirit, comes back into his body, and all that is dead and decayed comes back to life, and he walks out of that tomb alive and well! (See John 11:1-44.)

Jesus doesn't listen to the discouraging voices declaring death and that it's too late to hope for a miracle. Instead He follows the voice of hope within Himself that firmly believes with God all things are possible. And He activates His faith and does the unthinkable—raises His friend from the dead.

FOLLOWING AFTER GOD'S VOICE

Faith recognizes and follows after the voice of God. In John 10:27 we read what Jesus, the Good Shepherd, says about His sheep, us: *"My sheep hear My voice, and I know them, and they follow Me."*

The mature believer knows God's voice, and can hear Him clearly whether it be through God's Word, through the inner voice, or by an audible voice. We hear God and willfully follow after Him and His ways.

And in light of what we've been talking about, it is very important that we recognize the voice of Jesus and not be confused when a lying spirit tries to deceive us with a deceptive message.

The voice of Jesus is full of hope, and His is the voice we want to follow.

WILL GOD SPEAK AGAINST HIS WORD?

How often have I heard people say that God spoke to them and told them something that was contrary to His Word. I ask you, "Will God speak against His Word?" No, He won't. Why not?

> *God is not human, that he should lie, not a human being, that he should change his mind. Does he speak and then*

not act? Does he promise and not fulfill? (Numbers 23:19 NIV).

According to Numbers 23:19, God is not human—He doesn't lie or change His mind. Because God spoke the following in Isaiah 53:5, *"By His stripes we are healed,"* we are assured that this is true. He made good on His healing promise at the whipping post, and purchased our healing for us with His all-powerful blood at the Cross.

Then why has your healing not manifested in your mortal body yet? Or why did it not manifest in your loved one? Tough questions, I agree. But Jesus makes it very clear to us over and over again throughout His Word that we are responsible to manifest our own healing. He says in Mark 16:17-18, *"And these signs will follow those who believe."* The answer to these difficult questions is in the believing.

Another well-known Scripture is found in Mark 11:23 (NIV) concerning faith, *"Truly I tell you, if anyone says to this mountain, 'Go, throw yourself into the sea,' and does not doubt in their heart but believes that what they say will happen, it will be done for them."* Just a little bit of faith, when activated for the right thing will cause that mountain in your life to obey your command.

God's Word does not change according to our feelings or experiences—good or bad. God does not say things to us that contradict His Word. He does not mislead us, nor does He speak to us with falsehoods. He is faithful to perform His Word. And in this case, He says that our faith heals us and makes us whole.

> *And He said to her, "Daughter, be of good cheer; your faith has made you well. Go in peace"* (Luke 8:48).

God's given us the responsibility to work our faith to the manifestation of our healing. So the issue is not God being unfaithful to perform His Word, but that we are unfaithful to believe what He says is true. This is why it is important that we read and study the Word until our level of faith matches biblical standards, so it produces what God intends for it to produce.

Let's pray.

> *Father God,*
>
> *We ask for Your forgiveness for our ignorance concerning Your promises to heal and make us whole in spirit, in soul, and in our physical body. Forgive us for putting faith in our feelings and experiences rather than in Your Word. We have lowered You to the standard of that of humans who lie and change their minds, instead of accepting the spiritual responsibility to bring forth the manifestation of our healing by the working of our faith. Forgive us and help us in the area of our unbelief so that we can believe as we should. In Jesus' name, we pray, amen.*

WE CAN BE VOICES OF HOPE

Instead of beating one another down with vocal clubs of despair, we can be voices of hope who lead people to the heavenly Father who loves us and is good. We can build them up in the faith with the truth found in God's healing promises. This truth, in Jesus' name, sets people free who are bound by a spirit of death.

In Second Kings 5 we read a wonderful example of a young servant girl who was a voice of hope for God and was used mightily in the life of Naaman, a commander of the army of Syria. In all the splendor of this position, he had a deadly problem, he was a leper. Leprosy was a contagious and incurable disease.

A message from the prophet Elisha was sent to the commander on how to be healed from this premature death. He was to dip in the Jordan River seven times and he would be healed. This message made him angry and he did not want to comply with this act of faith. But God used a young servant girl who was willing to be a voice of hope to speak plainly to Naaman. Her words of hope encouraged him to activate his faith. When he dipped in the Jordan for the seventh time, he came up delivered and cleansed from this deadly disease.

Like this young girl, you can be the voice of hope God can use to deliver someone from the spirit of death.

HOW TO PRAY WHEN TOLD THERE IS NO HOPE

A sister in the Lord writes, "Please pray for my friend. She was diagnosed with pancreatic cancer which has spread to her stomach. She's been given no hope to live."

How should we pray over a loved one when we are told there is no hope, such as this woman?

> *In the name of Jesus, I renounce this spirit of death, pancreatic cancer, and the cancer in the stomach. I curse it at its very root and seed. I release the healing power of the Holy Spirit to flow into her cellular realm and that all cancer cells are eliminated from the body and new cells are recreated and they are super healthy and cancer-free. I renounce all tumors and command them to shrivel up and not to grow back in the name of the Lord. I speak to all cells, tissues, organs, and systems to be healed and made whole for the glory of the Lord, amen and amen.*

THE GOD OF HOPE

I love this prayer prayed by the apostle Paul on our behalf found in Romans 15:13 (AMP), *"May the God of hope fill you with all joy and peace in believing [through the experience of your faith] that by the power of the Holy Spirit you will abound in hope and overflow with confidence in His promises."* It's uplifting to know that our Lord Jesus is the God of hope. Hope is the precursor to faith, and we can't have faith unless we first have hope, and we certainly can't have real hope without God. And our God of hope fills us with all joy and peace.

Again my heart rejoices as I take the time to meditate upon this thought that He fills us with all joy; in other words, He fills us with His supernatural strength. Nehemiah 8:10 tells us not to grieve, for *"the joy of the Lord is our strength."* Joy and strength go hand in hand, for you can't have one without the other. And He doesn't want to give us a little bit of joy, but *all* joy. He wills that we are happy and strong in Him.

Now this doesn't necessarily mean we are laughing all the time, but isn't it amazing how revitalized we are after a hearty laugh. I deal with the real hurts of people every day of my life, so I especially love how the Lord makes me laugh. He knows that I have to have a dose of His medicine—laughter every day of my life. See Proverbs 17:22.

This joy comes from knowing that whatever difficulties I experience, I have the peace of God that truly surpasses all human understanding and human intellect. This peace isn't based upon feelings and it's not an emotion—it's an intimate place in my relationship with God. The closer I am to Jesus, the stronger this peace is.

His joy and peace are spiritual benefits from believing in the Holy Spirit's power. For me it is reassuring that God doesn't expect us to do His work in our own strength, but in His. Zechariah 4:6 reassures us that it is not by our might nor by our power, but by His Spirit. The power of His Spirit empowers us daily, if we accept His might.

And it is by the power of His Spirit that we will abound in hope. Other ways to say abound with hope is to be full of hope, overflow with hope, teem with hope, or to be packed with hope. When I allow myself the time to ponder the message of the Word, my spiritual understanding deepens. I like the visual of my spirit being teamed with His hope by the power of Holy Spirit.

We can overflow with confidence in His promises to us. This is not about being confident in ourselves, but being totally confident in Him and in His faithfulness to keep His promises to us. Therefore, we can do as Hebrews 4:16 encourages us to do and come boldly to the throne of grace.

We've learned how we are to follow the voice of hope and why we can be hopeful in His faithfulness to us. Now, let's turn to the next chapter and discuss how we overcome by the power of His blood.

A Declaration of Faith to Pray

Father God, I declare by faith that You are my God, and that You truly do care for my need. You love me, and want me to come boldly before Your throne of grace. You are able and willing to deliver me from a spirit of death and to heal my body, too. I do not need to suffer—I need to believe and receive my healing, in Your loving name, I pray, amen.

Pledge

I pledge to God and to myself to follow after the voice of hope. To learn to discern when a lying spirit is trying to manipulate me to believe that God's love has failed me, or that tries to get me to fall into its trap that God doesn't care to meet my need. I know better. I know the truth that He always loves me; even when I am at my worst, He loves me as if I were at my best. His voice I will follow, whether He speaks to me through His Word, by the inner voice, or by an audible voice. I know it's of Him because He never contradicts His Holy Scriptures—the Bible.

Questions for Chapter 11—Following the Voice of Hope

1. Spiritually speaking, what is unnatural for us?

2. What type of beings are we?

3. How do we arrive at the level of faith where we don't doubt Him and His ways?

4. Even when we are at our worst, how does God love us?

5. How does the world see?

6. How does God see us?

7. What is the power working within us that activates His generosity toward us?

8. Regardless of how impossible the situation looks, the Lord is what?

9. What does Hebrews 4:16 tell us about coming to Him with a need?

10. What happens when people lack hope and the understanding that God loves them?

11. In order to follow after the voice of hope, we have to be able to do what?

12. Is there any place in God's Word that tells us to give up and die?

13. What does faith recognize and follow?

14. Will God speak something contrary to His Word?

15. What is the issue if it's not God being unfaithful to perform His Word?

16. Instead of beating one another down with vocal clubs of despair, we can be what?

17. What can we overflow with?

Personal Reflection

Am I following the voice of hope? Or am I allowing lying spirits to deter me away from His message of hope? Have I entered into the arena of fear and despair about the present situation? If I have, am I willing to return to the right track with God and hear His voice of hope again?

Group Discussion

Today, let's talk about following the voice of hope. Have we been following this voice? Or have we been listening to lying spirits concerning our present situation? Do we need to spend more time in God's Word to be able to better discern the voice of hope? Will God speak against His Word? Do my personal beliefs concerning His healing promises need some adjusting? Let's get real and honest with one another and discuss these issues.

Chapter 12

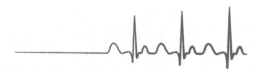

OVERCOMING BY THE
BLOOD OF THE LAMB

WORD OF THE LORD

The Lord would say to you this day, "I, the Lord God would say to you, I have given to you the power of My blood. Apply it liberally to every situation you face. It has been given to you at a high price, but to you it is freely given. Don't take this free gift for granted—learn to value My blood and the power it possesses for you. I love you with an everlasting love, and I gave everything I possibly could for you—Myself. And in Me are the many benefits you need to overcome the enemy in this late hour. Reach out and activate My power."

There isn't any power stronger than the blood of Jesus. And we owe it to ourselves and to those we love to have a strong understanding of this power.

When we study the Bible concerning the power of the blood, we read spiritual terms such as atonement, sanctification, justified, grace, and redemption. But what do these terms mean? And in what ways do they benefit us today?

ATONEMENT

Atonement is the reconciliation between God and people by the sacrificial offering of Jesus' blood at Calvary. Back in Bible days, people had to sacrifice, shedding the blood of bulls and goats to purify their flesh from their sinful ways—but then Jesus Christ offered Himself as the supreme sacrifice to cleanse us from all unrighteousness.

> *For if the blood of bulls and goats and the ashes of a heifer, sprinkling the unclean, sanctifies for the purifying of the flesh, how much more shall the blood of Christ, who through the eternal Spirit offered Himself without spot to God, cleanse your conscience from dead works to serve the living God?* (Hebrews 9:13-14)

We receive the power of His atoning blood by faith. We ask Him to forgive us of our sins. And the Bible assures us in First John 1:9, *"If we confess our sins, He is faithful and just to forgive us our sins and to cleanse us from all unrighteousness."* It's His shed blood that covers us, and reconciles us with Father God.

SANCTIFICATION

> *Do you not know that the unrighteous will not inherit the Kingdom of God? Do not be deceived. Neither fornicators, nor idolaters, nor adulterers, nor homosexuals, nor sodomites, nor thieves, nor covetous, nor drunkards, or revilers, nor extortioners will inherit the Kingdom of God. But when you accepted Jesus as your Lord and Savior, you were washed, you were sanctified, and you were justified*

in the name of the Lord Jesus and by the Spirit of our God (1 Corinthians 6:9-11).

Hebrews 13:12 tells us that we are sanctified by the blood. "Sanctification" comes from the Greek word *hagiazō*, and it means to make holy, purify, or to consecrate (Strong's G37). The blood of Jesus purifies us and makes us holy onto Him. His blood consecrates us; in other words, it separates us from our sinful nature and sets us apart for Him.

JUSTIFIED, GRACE, AND REDEMPTION

For all have sinned and fall short of the glory of God, being justified freely by His grace through the redemption that is in Christ Jesus, whom God set forth as a propitiation by His blood, through faith, to demonstrate His righteousness, because in His forbearance God had passed over the sins that were previously committed, to demonstrate at the present time His righteousness, that He might be just and the justifier of the one who has faith in Jesus (Romans 3:23-26).

"Justified" comes from the Greek word, *dikaioō*, and it means to render just or innocent—free (Strong's G1344). "Grace" is from the Greek word *charis*, and means good will, lovingkindness, and favor (Strong's G5485). And "redemption" comes from the Greek word *apolytrōsis*, and it means a releasing effected by payment of ransom (Strong's G629).

These are very powerful terms, and it is by His grace, His good will, lovingkindness, and favor that He willfully poured out His blood for us at Calvary to pay the ransom for our sinful ways, to redeem us, to pay for our justification in Him, and to deliver us from satan and all of his wicked works. It's the blood of our Savior Jesus Christ that frees us and sets us apart from all unrighteous acts.

185

SEVEN MAJOR BENEFITS PURCHASED BY THE POWER OF THE BLOOD

1. **Forgiveness of Sins**. *"Repent therefore and be converted, that your sins may be blotted out, so that times of refreshing may come from the presence of the Lord"* (Acts 3:19).

2. **Redemption**. *"In Him we have redemption through His blood, the forgiveness of sins, according to the riches of His grace"* (Ephesians 1:7).

3. **Deliverance**. *"They triumphed over him by the blood of the Lamb and by the word of their testimony; they did not love their lives so much as to shrink from death"* (Revelation 12:11 NIV).

4. **Eternal Life**. *"For God so loved the world that He gave His only begotten Son, that whoever believes in Him should not perish but have everlasting life"* (John 3:16).

5. **Abundant Life**. *"I have come that they may have life, and that they may have it more abundantly"* (John 10:10).

6. **Supernatural Healing**. *"Bless the Lord, O my soul, and forget not all His benefits: Who forgives all your iniquities, who heals all your diseases"* (Psalm 103:2-3).

7. **Divine Protection**. *"But the Lord is faithful and will strengthen you and protect you from the evil one"* (2 Thessalonians 3:3 NIV).

Forgiveness of Sins

What a blessing it is to have our sins forgiven us—to be free from the negative consequences of them. Because of the blood that was shed for us, we can be free from the curse of satan and all of his wicked works. We can stand boldly before God, free from all guilt and shame of past mistakes. No longer does anything stand between us and our Lord. Forgiveness is a free gift of God, and it is for anyone willing to receive it.

> *Repent therefore and be converted, that your sins may be blotted out, so that times of refreshing may come from the presence of the Lord* (Acts 3:19).

Redemption

So rich is God's grace toward us in that He sent His Son, Jesus, to redeem us, to release us from the consequences of what we truly deserved—death and damnation. But praise Jesus He paid our debt in full with His all-powerful blood. And for those who believe upon the Lord Jesus and receive His grace of redemption, we are now free.

Deliverance

Hell is an actual place—an eternal land of inconceivable loneliness, suffering, and torment. It is reserved for those who refuse to receive Jesus as their Savior. God does not desire for anyone to spend their eternity there, but He allows us the choice of a free will. Where will we choose to spend our eternity? The closer we are to the Lord's return, the harder the enemy is at war against people to keep them from the loving arms of our heavenly Father and an eternity in Heaven with our Savior. The demonic forces are out in full force to lead people astray from the truth that will set them free, and into a living hell on this earth full of filthy bondage.

My husband and I and our ministry partner and family friend Palma, were asked to make an emergency house call to a brother in the Lord who had opened himself up to the suffering and torment of satan and his demons. He got caught up in the sin of pornography that led him to utter bondage and misery.

He was in a demonic state of mind, emotionally and physically. His wife and family had been fighting for his life as this demon declared it would not leave until he and his family were destroyed.

The man was not himself anymore. He was possessed and violent toward his wife, screaming lies at her, blaming her for his sinful choices. It had the man at the point of death, collapsing to the ground barely able to breathe. He had been taken to the hospital numerous times over the past week, and the doctors were unable to help him. Why? Because even though this attack was manifesting in the natural realm and harming him physically, the problem was spiritual and had to be dealt with spiritually.

We were called to go and minister reconciliation over him. We arrived to find him lying on his bed as if he were dead. We laid our healing hands upon him and immediately, while unresponsive to normal interaction with other people, his fists clinched tightly around his covers. We continued to pray in the Spirit, in tongues, and the demon within him awakened and started to violently scream at his wife. I shielded his wife and took her out of the room.

We continued to pray in our supernatural languages, and the man stood up unaware of what was going on, leaning on my husband. The demon was very angry, but we just kept on praying in tongues. And then came the breakthrough this man needed—deliverance through repentance.

> So from now on we regard no one from a worldly point of view. Though we once regarded Christ in this way, we do so no longer. Therefore, if anyone is in Christ, the new creation has come: The old has gone, the new is here! All this is from God, who reconciled us to himself through Christ and gave us the ministry of reconciliation: that God was reconciling the world to himself in Christ, not counting people's sins against them. And he has committed to us the

message of reconciliation. We are therefore Christ's ambassadors, as though God were making his appeal through us. We implore you on Christ's behalf: **Be reconciled to God**. *God made him who had no sin to be sin for us, so that in him we might become the righteousness of God* (2 Corinthians 5:16-21 NIV).

We led the man in a prayer of repentance to God, asking his wife to forgive him. Even though the man was physically weak, he was at peace and calm. We helped him lay down on his bed to sleep. Later on that evening he called my husband for further counsel and prayer.

> *For if, while we were God's enemies, we were reconciled to him through the death of his Son, how much more, having been reconciled, shall we be saved through his life!* (Romans 5:10)

While we were praying in the Spirit, the Lord showed me a vision of what was taking place during this time of deliverance. I was shown a pit of fire; the flames were very large and hot. As we continued to minister over the man by praying in tongues, I saw hands reach down into the fiery pit of hell and lift this man by the scruff of his neck out of the flames.

Use the gift of tongues that the Lord has so richly given to His people and pray your loved ones out of the fiery pit of hell.

If ever there was a time, it is now for us, the ambassadors of Christ, to follow His example and be about our heavenly Father's business. We must return to the true gospel message of the redemptive blood of Jesus Christ and preach and minister with His authority with signs and wonders following and the captives set free.

> *The Spirit of the Lord is upon Me, because He has anointed Me to preach the gospel to the poor; He has sent Me to heal*

the brokenhearted, to proclaim liberty to the captives and recovery of sight to the blind, to set at liberty those who are oppressed; to proclaim the acceptable year of the Lord (Luke 4:18-19).

Eternal Life

Regardless of what society tries to tell us, both Heaven and hell are real physical places. And when we die, our spirit being will pass into eternity to either one of these places depending on the decision we make—to believe in Jesus as our Savior, or to reject Him.

God does not will for anyone to perish, to go to hell, so He sent His Son, Jesus, Yeshua, to suffer and die for us on the Cross to pay for our sins, our disobedience against God and His ways. He came to this earth and paid for our sins and the consequences of our sins with His most precious blood.

And now you decide where you will spend your eternity, either Heaven or hell. In Heaven you will have the reward of blessing to live with Jesus for eternity. Or you will spend your eternity suffering with your enemy, satan. The decision is up to you.

The Bible tells us in Romans 10:9-10 *"that if you confess with your mouth the Lord Jesus and believe in your heart that God has raised Him from the dead, you will be saved. For with the heart one believes unto righteousness, and with the mouth confession is made unto salvation."*

First, believe in your heart that Jesus is who the Bible says He is. Then when you believe this, confess, say with your mouth that you believe in Him.

When you take these two all-important steps in life, you are instantly a member of God's eternal family. God calls you, "born again."

You know you have a decision to make; if you believe in your heart that Jesus is who the Bible says He is, you are ready to make a decision to follow Him. Let's pray.

> *Dear Father God,*
>
> *Yes, I do believe. Jesus, You are the one and only way to salvation. I ask You to forgive me of my sins and come into my life and be my Savior and Lord. I thank You that I am forgiven, and I am born again this day. I am blessed to be part of Your eternal family. I love You, amen.*

If you've prayed with a sincere heart, you are now born again and a member of God's eternal family. Welcome to the family of God!

> *These things I have written to you who believe in the name of the Son of God, that you may know that you have eternal life, and that you may continue to believe in the name of the Son of God* (1 John 5:13).

Abundant Life

No longer do we need to suffer a life of poverty, death to our daily provision. All of our daily needs can be met by His redeeming blood. His Word promises us in Philippians 4:19, *"And my God shall supply all your need according to His riches in glory by Christ Jesus."* No matter the earthly economy or what's in your bank account, God is able to supply all of your needs according to His riches. And let's face it, there are many things in this life that money cannot buy such as deliverance from a spirit of death, a recreated body part, and an inner healing of the soul, just to name a few of the things earthly currency cannot purchase.

How do we activate His provision? We do so by faith.

Matthew 6:26 asks us a thought-provoking question, *"Look at the birds of the air, for they neither sow nor reap nor gather into barns; yet your heavenly Father feeds them. Are you not of more value than they?"* He encourages us not to worry about what we are going to eat, to drink, or about what we are going to wear. And then verse 33 tells us the plan to bring life back into the flow of His daily provision in our lives, *"But seek first the kingdom of God and His righteousness, and all these things shall be added to you."*

As with any of God's promises, we have a part to play to access His provision. Malachi 3:10 reveals to us how to open the windows of Heaven so blessings pour over us:

> *Bring all the tithes into the storehouse, that there may be food in My house, and try Me now in this," Says the Lord of hosts, "If I will not open for you the windows of heaven and pour out for you such blessing that there will not be room enough to receive it."*

Luke 6:38 instructs us how to secure God's provision: *"Give, and it will be given to you: good measure, pressed down, shaken together, and running over will be put into your bosom. For with the same measure that you use, it will be measured back to you."*

We may not understand how God does this, and we don't need to. We just need to be obedient to His Kingdom ways. I have learned in life—you can never out-give God.

Supernatural Healing

The shed blood of our precious Jesus provides supernatural healing for us. This is good news that should be shared with all people. As I travel around the world, I have never seen God's people as sick as they are now. The culprit for this is the lack of teaching about the redemptive blood of Jesus to heal the sick. Hosea 4:6 tells us that God's people perish for a lack of knowledge.

Many churches no longer offer the message of healing to their congregants. And when these people are attacked by the enemy with one of his major weapons of sickness and disease, they fall ill, and often gravely ill, with no hope in the natural to get better—most are certainly not offered a prayer of faith for healing.

The supernatural healing power of Jesus is a good and perfect gift that comes from God. When the blind see, the deaf hear, the mute speak, and the paralytics walk, it's a time to celebrate the goodness of our Jehovah Rapha, our God who heals us. When a cancerous tumor disappears, or a defective heart is supernaturally recreated, it's time to rejoice.

Healing is a great gift that is meant to be shared. And not only are the lives of the recipients of these miracles forever changed, but so too are those who hear of these testimonies.

Three Healing Scriptures to Learn and Share

> *"For I will restore health to you and heal you of your wounds," says the Lord* (Jeremiah 30:17).

> *He personally carried our sins in His body on the cross [willingly offering Himself on it, as on an altar of sacrifice], so that we might die to sin [becoming immune from the penalty and power of sin] and live for righteousness; for by His wounds you [who believe] have been healed* (1 Peter 2:24 AMP).

> *...He Himself took our infirmities and bore our sicknesses* (Matthew 8:17).

Divine Protection

Have you ever had a near miss with death? Did you recognize the hand of God's protection? Or did you brush it off as mere coincidence? Let's consider the hand of God's protection over us for a moment.

And let me add here before I share two quick but power-filled testimonies that the fifth place Jesus shed His blood for us was through His hands, when He allowed them to pierce His hands to that old wooden Cross. When His blood was shed through those precious hands, He released the blessing to us. And the blessing includes divine protection by the power of the blood.

This testimony happened quite a few years ago, when we were living in a suburb of Guatemala City in Guatemala and our son, Micah, was still in high school at the time. He was walking home from a friend's house, minding his own business, when out of nowhere a stray bullet whizzed right past his head. Had he walked less than a half a step faster, that bullet would have hit him in the head. Was this just a close call?

A few years later we were living at the end of a village, and I was going for a walk with my babies, Jorge, Joaquin, Andres, and Marcos, with a few of the older kids from the children's home. We were talking away and hadn't even stepped off of our property yet when a stray bullet whizzed right past my face. Had I bent over even slightly, I too would have been shot in the head. Was this just another one of those coincidences? Or was something else unseen taking place at this moment?

As I explained in Chapter 8, we are living in perilous times, and the enemy knows his time is short. He fears God's people and the potential we all possess to share Jesus with the lost and hurting around us. So he and his spirit of death are taking cheap potshots at us, trying to take us out before our time. Remember, this is what he does best—steals, kills, and destroys. (See John 10:10.)

I believe that as those bullets were shot aimlessly by careless people, our enemy was taking advantage of these free-flying weapons and aimed them right at us, to do us harm. And the moment those bullets were shot in the air, God's hand of protection went up and over us. What the enemy uses for harm against us, the prayer of faith changes for good and for God's glory.

The prayer of faith founded by the blood of Jesus releases His divine protection over us when we need it. This is one reason why it is so important to live a lifestyle of prayer. Pray the Word daily over yourself and those you love.

And let me ask you one thought-provoking question concerning the time this protection was released. Was God's hand of protection released right before those bullets were about to hit us? I don't think so. Please hear me out on this point. I believe this was God's faith in action to my prayer of faith long before this incident ever took place. With all my heart, I believe God's mighty hand of protection went up to protect us from those flying bullets every time I prayed a declaration of faith that no weapon formed against me and my family will prosper in Jesus' name.

I daily plead the power of His blood over my family. Whenever the enemy whispers a negative thought against their safety, I immediately say, "No! In Jesus' name this will not happen to them. I plead the power of the blood of Jesus over them." I have been claiming the protection of the blood for forty years now, and I will continue to do so until He calls me home.

Three Divine Protection Scriptures to Learn and Share

No weapon formed against you shall prosper... (Isaiah 54:17).

The Lord also will be a refuge for the oppressed, a refuge in times of trouble. And those who know Your name will put their trust in You; for You, Lord, have not forsaken those who seek You (Psalm 9:9-10).

Behold, I give you the authority to trample on serpents and scorpions, and over all the power of the enemy, and nothing shall by any means hurt you (Luke 10:19).

We've built up our faith in the power of the blood and discussed why it is so important in these last days to make sure to pray the prayer of faith over ourselves and our families daily. Now, let's look to the next topic and talk about the power of declaring and praising our way out of premature death.

Prayer

> *Father God,*
>
> *In the name of Jesus, I am thankful for the power of the blood that was freely given to me. I admit I have taken it for granted. And for that I am truly sorry. I do not want to take the benefits that Your Son Jesus suffered to give to me. Help me Holy Spirit to appreciate and value the power of the blood. Help me to real-ize the hour in which I live and protect myself and my family with declarations of faith concerning the blood. In Jesus' name I pray, amen.*

Pledge

I pledge to God and myself to study the Scriptures to gain a deep understanding about the power of the blood. And to count my blessings of the seven benefits I have been given by the power of the blood: forgiveness of my sins, redemption, deliverance, eternal life, abundant life, supernatural healing, and divine protection in these last days.

Questions for Chapter 12—Overcoming by the Blood of the Lamb

1. What is atonement?

2. "Sanctification" comes from what Greek word? What does it mean?

3. In regard to sanctification, what does the blood of Jesus do for us?

4. "Justified" comes from what Greek word? What is its meaning?

5. *Charis* is the Greek word for what? What does it mean?

6. "Redemption" comes from what word in the Greek language? What does it mean?

7. What are the seven major benefits purchased by the power of the blood? Forgiveness is a free gift of God, but who is it for?

8. Redemption releases us from what consequences that we deserve?

9. As ambassadors of Christ, we are to follow His example to do what?

10. According to Romans 10:9-10, what two things must we do to be saved?

11. What are three things that earthly currency cannot buy?

12. According to Philippians 4:19, how shall God supply all your needs?

13. What is the reason God's people perish as revealed in Hosea 4:6?

14. What was the declaration of faith I prayed that protected us from the flying bullets?

Personal Reflection

After reading the section about divine protection, how do I feel about this? Is there a time when I know God's hand of protection prevented death in a given situation? Have I been declaring words of faith for my protection and the protection of my family? If not, am I willing to start doing so now?

Group Discussion

Read aloud the testimony under the subtitle, Divine Protection. Discuss it together. What are the feelings among the group about what I said concerning the timing the actual protection was released, "With all my heart, I believe God's mighty hand of protection went up to protect us from those flying bullets every time I prayed a declaration of faith *that no weapon formed against me and my family will prosper in Jesus' name."* Then ask others in the group to share similar incidents when they know God's hand of protection prevented death in a given situation.

Chapter 13

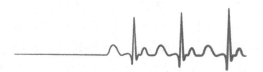

DECLARING AND PRAISING YOUR WAY OUT OF PREMATURE DEATH

Have you ever stopped to think about the power of your speech? According to Proverbs 18:21, you have the power of life and death in your tongue. That's amazing strength, and not to be taken lightly. Consider the possibilities your miracle-working words possess. With all this power in your tongue, perhaps it would be worthwhile to choose words with care.

Death and life are in the power of the tongue, and those who love it will eat its fruit (Proverbs 18:21).

Every day we are given opportunities to release the power of life and death with our words. According to God's Word what we say really matters. What are we saying? What should we say? And what should we not say?

The one who has knowledge uses words with restraint, and whoever has understanding is even-tempered. Even fools are thought wise if they keep silent, and discerning if they hold their tongues (Proverbs 17:27-28 NIV).

If we will learn how to hold our tongues, we will keep ourselves from a heap of unnecessary troubles.

Those who guard their mouths and their tongues keep themselves from calamity (Proverbs 21:23 NIV).

The power of our speech runs deep into the affairs of life and our words can be life-giving. Are we using them in a godly and mature manner? Are we producing what God desires us to produce—life?

The words of a man's mouth are like deep waters [copious and difficult to fathom]; the fountain of [mature, godly] wisdom is like a bubbling stream [sparkling, fresh, pure, and life-giving] (Proverbs 18:4 AMP).

SPEAK LIKE JESUS SPOKE

I believe the Word of God when it says that as Jesus is, so are we on this earth (see 1 John 4:17). Jesus was a Man filled with faith when He walked this earth in human form. He lived like we live. He faced daily trials and temptations, yet He did not sin. He was not a con artist. He did not try to pull the wool over the eyes of the people. He was an honest Man, and His heart was pure, free from sin, and full of love and compassion for all people. He came to show us how to live by faith according to the Father's ways.

Take time to ponder upon this thought for a moment—*as Jesus is, so are we on this earth*. What an amazing word from God! We are to emulate Him, act like Him, love like Him, and even speak like Him. And just how does He speak? With all authority He speaks. He was not passive with His words. He always spoke with a purpose. His words cut to the heart of the matter. He rebuked the religious, was compassionate with the hurting, and He put satan and his demons in their place everytime. Even as a child He was speaking in the realm of the prophetic.

He has a way with His words that dramatically alters the lives of those He comes into contact with, and so should we. We are to be like Him and use this gift, the power of the spoken word, to prophesy healing to all those in need in our arena of influence. Romans 4:17 teaches us to *"call those things which do not exist as though they did"*—this is prophesying. And it is not as mysterious as some might think. We do it all the time; every time we open our mouths, we prophesy either life or death (see Proverbs 18:21).

With all of this in mind, perhaps we should learn to use this supernatural power, the gift of the spoken language, in such a way that we create a change and alter the destinies of the people around us for the glory of God. Learn how to surrender our words to Him, and allow the Holy Spirit to play a vibrant melody on the strings of our vocal chords.

Let's choose to speak like Jesus spoke—full of authority and power—and alter the circumstances around us for His glory.

CHOOSE TO LIVE AND NOT TO DIE

We live in a fallen world and we have an enemy that is out to harm us in whatever way he possibly can. This is why we need to be firm in our decision to live and fulfill our destiny on this earth.

There was a time when I was really sick and running a high fever. The fever was so high that the bed was literally shaking from my trembling. I was in a lot of pain. But I had the will to live. Even with my head in the toilet vomiting violently, I was declaring, "I will not die, but live in the name of Jesus!"

I had a large kidney stone and they wanted to operate immediately to remove it. I told them, "No." Even though it was a painful battle, I was healed supernaturally from it.

My point in sharing this short testimony is this, we have to *choose* to live, and not to die.

CHOOSE TO NOT GIVE UP

Not to give up is a decision that we all have to choose from time to time. And it can be one of the hardest decisions we will ever have to make. To continue to fight the enemy is really tough, and it takes every ounce of faith within you to do so. Especially when we are dealing with life and death situations. For Christians, we know that when we die we pass into eternity with Christ, and that is a wonderful occasion. But we need to ask ourselves if have we fulfilled God's destiny for us on earth. And does the situation line up with the Word of God?

Is it the Father's plan that people die while young, or prematurely? What does His Word tell us? *"For I know the plans I have for you,' declares the Lord, 'plans to prosper you and not to harm you, plans to give you hope and a future'"* (Jeremiah 29:11 NIV). Premature death robs people from their future, so it does not come from God.

So when the enemy tempts you to give up the good fight of faith, don't listen to him. Instead, call upon the strength of the Lord when you feel weak and allow His strength to take over for you. Remember, *choose to not give up.*

KNOW GOD'S WILL TO HEAL YOU

How many times have I heard someone say that it is not always God's will to heal all people. Or that He chooses to heal some, but not all. Comments like these are like fingernails scratching on a chalkboard to me. They cause my spirit to cringe, and they should cause yours to cringe as well. Let's turn to the Scriptures to discover the truth about God's will to heal us.

Jesus had to deal with this issue as well; one such time is recorded in the Book of Luke 5:12-13:

> *And it happened when He was in a certain city, that behold, a man who was full of leprosy saw Jesus; and he fell on his face and implored Him, saying, "Lord, if You are willing, You can make me clean." Then He put out His hand and touched him, saying, "I am willing; be cleansed." Immediately the leprosy left him.*

Let's study these verses out a bit more to see the depth of the desire He has to heal us. The leprous man called out, *"If You are willing."* This word "willing" in Greek is *thelō* (Strong's Concordance G2309) and it means to will, to have in mind, to intend, to be resolved, to be determined, to purpose, to desire, to wish, to love, or to like to do a thing. This man inquired of Jesus, "Do You desire to heal me? Is it Your purpose or intent to heal me? Would You love to heal me?" Perhaps you desire to understand the intent of Jesus concerning healing. And you, like this man want to know, "Is it His will to heal me?"

Shall we continue on to find out what His will is in this matter? Not only does this man want to know if Jesus is willing, but he wants to know if He can heal him. The word "can" in Greek is *dynamai* (Strong's G1410) and it means able, powerful and strong. He wants to put an end to his doubt and find out if Jesus possesses the ability to heal, because in the natural his situation is labeled impossible and carries the power of death and suffering. This man's life depends on a miracle, and is Jesus the One who is strong and powerful and able and willing to give him this much needed miracle?

You may be wondering the same, *Is His strength and power greater than the disease attacking my body? Does He really possess the ability to make my body whole again?*

This man was seeking Jesus for deep truths about His credentials, "Can He make me clean?" This word "make" in Greek is *katharizō* and means to cleanse, to purge, and to purify (Strong's G2511). This man is plagued with a curse of death and needs to be purged from it. To purge yourself from something is to be free from something unwanted. This man needed to be completely free from leprosy; no residue of it could remain in his body if he were to be totally free and cleansed from it.

Are you in this man's situation? Your body needs to be purged from sickness or disease, and not a trace of it can remain.

In response to this man's plea for a miracle, Jesus does the unthinkable, what others are afraid to do—He reaches out and touches the man. Let's ponder upon the faith principles that are being activated at this point in time. Jesus is demonstrating to us how we are to be by His example on earth in the form of a human being. He was operating in the principles of faith, and faith operates by love, and love alone, and there is no fear in faith.

> *For in Christ Jesus neither circumcision nor uncircumcision avails anything, but faith working through love* (Galatians 5:6).

> *There is no fear in love; but perfect love casts out fear, because fear involves torment. But he who fears has not been made perfect in love* (1 John 4:18).

Jesus answers the man suffering with leprosy, *"I am willing."* Meaning, I desire to heal you. I would love to heal you. My intention is to heal, and not to harm you. And this is what He is saying to you as well.

DO YOU HAVE THE WILL TO LIVE?

He wills to heal you, but do you have the will to live? Yes, it's difficult to fight this fight against the spirit of death, but have you taken the time and considered how hard it was for Him to take not only this disease, but the diseases of all people upon His body? He didn't give up. He fought hard, was tortured for our victory, so we could be delivered from the spirit of death and healed from all sickness and disease.

Because He did it first, we can now follow in His footprints mapped out for us in the Word of God. We can overcome the spirit of death; we can learn how to believe, put all doubt and unbelief far from us, and obtain our healing and miracle from God.

THE VALLEY OF THE SHADOW OF DEATH

> *Yea, though I walk through the valley of the shadow of death, I will fear no evil; for You are with me; Your rod and Your staff, they comfort me* (Psalm 23:4).

I was in Malawi, Africa, ministering to a woman who was in the last stages of HIV/AIDS in a coma dying. I pulled up a chair so I could be near her ear and I began to speak to her a word of encouragement filled with hope for her future. I renounced the spirit of death and all that was killing her body. I then released the Spirit of Life, and the power of the Holy Spirit to flow in and throughout her body. I told her to wake up in the name of Jesus, but nothing happened. The Holy Spirit quickened to my mind that she was in the valley of the shadow of death and she needed to make a decision to turn around and come back to fulfill her life on earth. I shared with her what the Spirit had just shared with me. I said to her, "I have done everything I can do. Now, it's up to you to choose to live and come back to life."

No sooner had these words left my lips, when she grabbed hold of my arm, turned her head, and looked me straight in the eye. She woke up out of the coma that she had been in for days. I turned to her mother and her aunt who were with us in the room and said, "She's made her decision to come back and fulfill her life on earth. Now, you love on her, encourage her, and give her a reason to live."

You might be in a similar situation and you too need to choose to live and walk out of the valley of the shadow of death.

DECLARED AND PRAISED AWAY A CANCEROUS TUMOR

I want to share with you a wonderful testimony from an amazing woman of faith and how she by faith declared and praised away a cancerous tumor.

On January 14, 2019, I received the following prayer request from Theresa.

> Dear Becky, I am the mother of 4, and am waiting for a triple biopsy. The doctors said it's cancer in the breast and lymph glands, left side, a sudden and spontaneous appearance. I would like to accept an immediate healing on the power of The Word that all that was found will be found no more. I reject this entirely and ask for God's glory to stun, baffle and soften the doctors surrounding me, and that my husband and children can see the living power of our God. I will sing His praises with my stringed instrument, with the voice He gave me, in the songs that His Spirit sends, in a body made

whole, just as He created, free of satan's latest attack! Please pray prophetically for me. Let His Glory be raised up! Amen.

My response to her that day.

Dearest Teresa, In the name of Jesus I join my faith with your prophetic utterance over yourself. I renounce the spirit of death coming against you and the reports of cancer. We dare to believe the report of the Lord that declares by His stripes you are already healed. I renounce these cancer reports, cancer cells, cancer tumors at their seed. I command them to dry up at their roots and die off and be eliminated from your body. They may not come back. And I declare new cells that are cancer-free, strong and healthy for the glory of our Lord Jesus Christ, amen and amen. I am standing with you.

January 15, 2019

Becky, I'm getting it. Watching your videos on YouTube. I have allowed the enemy control over my reaction to attacks on our family to derail us from God's purposes for my husband, myself, and our children. The devil is shooting for premature death and using my own words spoken in anger against me. No one has ever taught us what you are teaching us, and it's in the Bible. Becky, stand in the gap with me in prophetic prayer. I am weak, but I will stand in faith believing and trust receiving. The power of satan will be broken right now in Jesus' name, from our lives, and every infectious disease cancer gone now in the name of Jesus. There is no place for any of this in our temples. It's more than cancer going away. The chains that have bound our service and fruits in the Kingdom are going away too. I claim this in Jesus' name.

Please keep praying. This is a super battle for the glory of God. Love in Christ, Teresa

My response that day:

You've got it! Now speak life and life only. Hugs, Becky.

Messages on January 16, 2019

Teresa writes:

On the battlefield that's in my body, and now my son has a wound and the doctors don't know what it is. He had to undergo a biopsy. While I await a triple biopsy this Tuesday morning, my son gets one unexpectedly yesterday afternoon. We are both in pain and saying aloud, "We will be fine. God has already healed us." ...Though weak, we stand with only His Word as our strength. In faith believing. In trust receiving. The battle is against invisible foe. The physical attack is very real. And the victory is already God's.

My response to her after her email:

I am praying and standing with you. Watch your confession. Keep it up no matter what is going on. Hugs, Becky

January 19, 2019

From Teresa:

My doctors and friends are looking at me like "Poor girl!" to all of my replies, "I'm already healed in the name of Jesus." Test on Tuesday, results on Wednesday and there will be nothing there in Jesus' name. I am already healed!

My response: "I am standing with you in faith."

January 22, 2019

Becky, something is happening. Just had the triple biopsy and the large tumor in the underarm is completely gone. They couldn't find it. And the two on the breast are smaller. The doctors and the nurses are very confused. These things don't just go away like that. That was a large tumor in the lymph gland in the underarm. I'll get the results on Thursday. Keep praying with me.

I respond to her praise report, "Dear Teresa, I am so happy for you! Keep me posted."

January 23, 2019

Teresa writes:

Yep, the large lump in the underarm pit is definitely gone, along with its deep pain. It's just not there anymore! Just two more small spots and weakness to go. Plus I need to recoup from yesterday's probing and testing. It's definitely a miracle in progress, with zero explanation, at least from the scientific world. Big hugs from Nebraska!

January 24, 2019

Teresa catches a bad cold and starts to allow her feelings to dictate her.

Please pray with me. I am so weak, physically, emotionally, mentally, and spiritually. I can't stop crying, facing the results in a meeting with the doctor at 3 PM today. It feels like a walk up Calvary to me. Even with one big tumor missing. I'm so weenie! And I caught a cold to boot. I feel so sick. Offering all this up to God is way over my feeble human pay scale. Satan is attacking us. In Jesus' name, "Leave my son and me alone!" Please stand by the "Wimpy Mommy" in prayer. I'm binding these fierce attacks in the name of Jesus.

I respond to Teresa's negative message:

You are not to be like a wave tossed to and fro. You are to remain stable no matter how you feel. And faith is not a feeling. It is what you stand upon when there are no feelings. If you continue to declare that you are wimpy and feeble, you will be. Is this what you want? Do you really want victory or defeat? A cold may be miserable, but it certainly is not defeat. Make up your mind, woman of God.

Teresa responds to my light rebuke.

I'm dropping anchor. Putting on the armor of God and trading my wimpy for warrior. I may be weak, but I am a child of the King. I am claiming total healing. It worked for David, and he was a musician too. Thank you for that. I do not accept defeat. We have one missing big tumor, and two more to go. I am claiming strength, my rightful heritage as a child of God. Doing what your book, *The Prophetic and Healing Power of Your Words,* says to do, speak prophetically words of healing over myself. Taking back the steering wheel to my vessel in this storm, and evening the keel. Thank you.

January 25, 2019

The next day Teresa writes:

Lymph glands are normal, cleared, no cancer, nor signs of it. The 14 cm tumor is gone, plus 5 to 7 satellite lesions are gone. The 2 remaining spots on the breast are smaller now too. They are now stage 2 verses stage 3. And the doctors can't explain this. We have a fully documented miracle. The lump in my underarm is definitely gone. That one was big enough I could feel it, and it hurt. The pain is gone. And now it's just a normal underarm again. The only pain I have now is from the biopsy surgery itself, and I'm bandaged up, and use ice and an over-the-counter pain reliever for it.

I respond to her wonderful praise report:

I am so very happy for you! This is such wonderful news and it will inspire many people to trust God for their miracle. And pray for your doctor, this is hard for him. I have found miracles like this scare those who don't know the Lord and His miracle-working power. It's beyond the natural realm. Trust me, he's pondering it. He needs Jesus.

She responds a few days later with a report of all that happened to her.

The surgical biopsy was run on Jan. 22, 2019, using guided ultrasound. So between Jan. 3rd and Jan. 22, the cancerous tumor disappeared. The biopsy report, which I have a hard copy of, for all of the images, shows no lymph mass or tumor present, lymph glands clear, no cancer!

When the first ultrasound was run on Jan. 3rd, what was seen, found and annotated on the image, prompted a stat mammogram. After the ultrasound, the doctor came in and explained to my husband and me what he had just found. He was very concerned because of the large mass he had found, and could be felt by touching on the outside, in the lymph gland. This was in addition to the spots on the breast itself, but he was more concerned and worried about the mass in the glands, and the surrounding lesions. And he wanted an immediate mammogram.

The head doctor of radiology took my case. We came back a few days later, and he sat my husband and me down, and explained to us all of the images that had been taken. He was very concerned about the mass in the lymph gland, and surrounding lesions. He recommended a triple deep core surgical biopsy for the two spots on the breast, and a double one for the lymph gland mass, and citing he may pull two samples out of that one. My husband and I were shown this mass and surrounding lesions in great detail, as well as the other two spots.

During the surgical biopsy, when it came time to do the lymph biopsy (my husband was present for this procedure, and sitting right next to me, both of us facing the screen so we could follow the procedure as the doctor performed it, since we are both tech geeks and were really fascinated by the procedure. It was really interesting what they can do and watching it being done). Upon inserting the needle into the GPS coordinates afforded by the prior ultrasound, exact spot, which the doctor had previously noted, was large enough that they didn't have to insert any markers to find it. I could feel it with my fingers. The images were up on the screen for reference, so we could actually see the before and now images.

But something was gone. We saw it before everyone went silent. Something was not right, and there was dead silence. The doctor breathed and said, "They don't just disappear!" Which prompted him to start probing around with the biopsy needle to find the missing mass and the surrounding lesions. My husband and I watched with complete shock and awe, because we knew what God had done. So I started asking questions like "Where did it go?" and "Can those just disappear?" My questions were met with silence and not answered. This was unexplainable and there was no comment. The nurses were smiling and afterward showed us how the instrument used to extract tissue worked.

Focus was put on the other two spots, and "What we thought was there" was the only comment, and never brought up again for the remaining procedure. And the "What we thought was there" was completely documented in multiple images on two separate procedures and witnessed by the first doctor who ran the first ultrasound and stat mammogram, and his attending technician. And then the doctor who ran the biopsy, who was the head of radiology, prior to the biopsy being run, and these same images used as the reason he needed to do a deep tissue, possibly two, for the mass and surrounding lesions in the underarm area, to which it had clearly spread. I have the full set of images from all tests, along with their respective reports and biopsy results, on a clinical DVD.

Dear reader, this is what the power of our words of declaration and praise are capable of doing, if activated in the right manner. And just what is the right manner?

1. When receiving a serious medical report, take the situation to the Lord.

2. Find people of like faith to support you in your battle against the spirit of death.

3. With the power of your spoken words, curse (as in this case) the spirit of death, the seeds of all cancerous cells and tumors in the mighty name of Jesus—our Healer.

4. With the same power of the spoken word, release the healing power of the Holy Spirit into the cellular

realm, command all cancer-infected cells to dry up at the seed and be eliminated from the body.

5. Start declaring with your healing words creative miracles to take place, and that new cells are created and function 100% to produce life, and life in abundance.

6. Begin to praise and worship the Lord that His healing power is activated in your body.

7. Do not allow yourself the pleasure of self-pity and speak life and only life over your physical being, in the name of Jesus.

8. Be persistent and don't stop declaring your creative miracle.

We discussed the power of our words and the importance of declaring and praising your way out of premature death. Now as we turn to the next chapter, we will talk about facing the fear of death in these last days.

Prayer

> *Dear Holy Spirit,*
> *I see how important my words are and that I either prophesy life or death into my body or situation. I ask for Your help to put a guard on my mouth and to use my words wisely, and in a way that brings glory and honor to Your name, amen.*

Pledge

I pledge to God and to myself to choose life, and the will to live. With my words I will curse the spirit of death, and release the spirit of life. I will declare creative miracles into my body, and I will praise and worship the Lord that His healing power is activated in my body. I will not allow myself the pleasure of self-pity, but will be persistent and will not stop declaring my creative miracle into existence for the glory of the Lord.

Questions for Chapter 13—Declaring and Praising Your Way Out of Premature Death

1. According to Proverbs 18:21, our words possess what power?

2. According to Proverbs 17:27 how does the one who has knowledge and understanding use their words?

3. What happens to those who guard their mouths and tongues according to Proverbs 21:23?

4. According to Proverbs 18:4, what are the words of a person's mouth like?

5. First John 4:17 says as Jesus is so are _____.

6. According to Romans 4:17 what are we to call those things that do not exist?

7. According to our reading, every time we open our mouth what do we do?

8. We need to be firm in our decision to what?

9. What does premature death rob people of?

10. What is the Greek word for "willing"? What does it mean?

11. What is the Greek word for "can"? What does it mean?

12. The Greek word for "make" is what? What is its meaning?

13. What do you need to do if you receive a serious medical report?

14. What type of people should you find to support you in your battle against the spirit of death?

15. With the power of your spoken words, what do you do with the spirit of death?

16. With the same power of your spoken words, what do you need to release?

17. What do you need to start declaring with your healing words?

18. Why do I say to begin to praise and worship the Lord?

19. Do not allow yourself the pleasure of what?

20. When declaring your creative miracle, what do I say to do?

Personal Reflection

Am I using my words wisely? Are my words giving glory and honor to my God? Have I been prophesying life or death into my body? Or into my present situation. From the list of eight ways to declare and praise, where do I need to make some alterations for my healing miracle to manifest?

Group Discussion

With your group discuss the power of our words and the importance of guarding what we say. Share with one another how we either prophesy life or death into our physical bodies or into our present situation. If time allows, praise and worship the Lord together for His healing power to be activated in your bodies.

Chapter 14

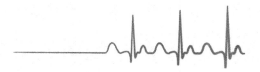

FACING THE FEAR OF DEATH IN THESE LAST DAYS

WORD OF THE LORD

The Lord would say to you this day, "Reach out to Me, My dear one. I am your Protector. I never sleep, and I never slumber. I go before you, I walk alongside you, and I take up your rear guard. Be not afraid this day, for I will never leave you, or forsake you. I am for you, and never against you. Be not dismayed by the hour that you live in. Yes, you live in turbulent times, and these things will be as they are prophesied in My Word. But now, more than ever, you must reach out to me. I will strengthen and protect you from the evil one. Keep your eyes fixed upon Me; I am faithful and true to you. When the enemy rushes in like a flood, it's time to raise up the standard of the blood. You overcome by the precious blood of the Lamb. And it is time for you to open your mouth and testify of the victorious day that soon will display all glory and splendor, for all who will humble themselves and pray, 'Come, Lord Jesus, come.'"

Do you fear tribulations, difficult times, persecution, and the uncertainty of the hour in which we live? What will happen with your job, your family, and your life? Are you afraid to stand up for Jesus because it may cost you your life? Do you sense the need for tighter security around you? Do you require more reassurance of the Lord's faithfulness? If so, you are not alone, many Christians struggle with the fear of death concerning these troubling times during these last days.

While traveling on a plane, there was terrible turbulence and many people around me were vomiting, and almost all were visibly praying. One woman was panicking and started shouting, "Get me off of here!" I have to be honest, at that moment I felt very vulnerable and fear was coming upon me. I placed my sweater over my face and started to pray in the Spirit. As I was praying in the Spirit, I heard the voice of the Lord say, *"Trust Me."* I immediately took control of this spirit of fear, renounced it, and started to pray in the Spirit, but in a different manner by taking control of the weather and calling forth ministering angels to guide us out of the storm.

How can we overcome these overwhelming feelings of fear and insecurity? One way we can calm our hearts is to pray, like I did while traveling through the turbulent skies. But don't pray mindless or faithless prayers, pray prayers of faith. Pray in tongues and pray prayers that include Scriptures from the Word of God.

I had to build myself up in the most holy faith and tell Him why I trusted Him, and pray in the Spirit. And in doing so I encouraged myself until I trusted in His strength to overcome, and not in the strength of the storm to overcome me.

WHY DO WE FEAR DEATH?

Why do we fear death? There is really no wrong answer to this question. But I bet people pretty much fear for the same reasons. Are we afraid we might find out what we believed in was wrong? Or perhaps we have regrets for not doing something we should have done. And maybe it's because we did something that we should not have done, and we fear that God might hold it against us. Perhaps we fear the unknown. And maybe we are just plain fearful of the pain death might bring. Whatever the reasons are, let's investigate them in God's Word and overcome these fears.

What if My Beliefs Are Wrong?

I think a lot of people fear this a bit more than they would like to admit. But the most important beliefs you must have to enter into eternal life with God is found in His Word in Romans 10:9-10:

> *If you confess with your mouth the Lord Jesus and believe in your heart that God has raised Him from the dead, you will be saved. For with the heart one believes unto righteousness, and with the mouth confession is made unto salvation.*

We are all in a growing process when it comes to our beliefs. The more we read the Word, the more we understand it. And I find that the Spirit of God is always challenging us in what we believe and why we believe it. We may see that some things we once believed were not biblical, and we will correct those wrong beliefs.

In Second Timothy 2:15, Paul challenges us with these words, *"Be diligent to present yourself approved to God, a worker who does not need to be ashamed, rightly dividing the word of truth."*

Steps to grow your faith:

1. Daily read the Bible.

2. Talk about its message with Him, and with others.

3. Speak His promises out loud.

4. Do what the Word tells you to do.

If you take these four steps of faith, you will find that your faith will grow.

I Have Regrets

You may fear death because you have regrets. This is true for many people. Be honest and ask yourself what you regret, and make the necessary changes now. You might say, "I can't undo them." You can always undo regretful things with the Lord by asking His forgiveness for them.

Always remember, *"He has not dealt with us according to our sins, nor punished us according to our iniquities. For as the heavens are high above the earth, so great is His mercy toward those who fear Him; as far as the east is from the west, so far has He removed our transgressions from us"* (Psalm 103:10-12).

I'm Afraid God Might Not Forgive Me

Perhaps you fear death because you fear that He might not forgive you. God assures us the following when it comes to His forgiveness toward us. Isaiah 1:18 says to us, *"'Come now, and let us reason together,' says the Lord, 'Though your sins are like scarlet, they shall be as white as snow; though they are red like crimson, they shall be as wool.'"*

Matthew 6:14-15 (NIV) clearly teaches us about forgiveness: *"If you forgive other people when they sin against you, your heavenly Father will also forgive you. But if you do not forgive others their sins, your Father will not forgive your sins."* You see, you are the one in control of God's forgiveness of your sins. Make sure you forgive people, whether they deserve it or not.

Right now, pray this prayer by faith and not by feelings:

> *Dear Father God, forgive me for not forgiving (name). Right now with Your help, I forgive (name), and I release this person from my bitterness and my vengeance. And in doing so, my sins are now forgiven, and I am free from bondage, in Jesus' name I pray, amen.*

If that old lying enemy tries to bring up hateful and unforgiving feelings about the people whom you have forgiven, rebuke him in the name of Jesus and tell him to be silent. And remind him and yourself what the Bible says, "I have forgiven (name), and God has forgiven me too."

Mark 3:28-30 (NIV) reveals to us the one sin that will not be forgiven us, "*Truly I tell you, people can be forgiven all their sins and every slander they utter, but whoever blasphemes against the Holy Spirit will never be forgiven; they are guilty of an eternal sin.' He said this because they were saying, 'He has an impure spirit.'*" The unpardonable sin is denying Jesus Christ as Lord and Savior. But you have the opportunity to change this now while you are alive.

As discussed earlier in the chapter, Romans 10:9-10 clearly lays out what we must do to be saved from eternal damnation—a life in hell with satan and all of his demons for eternity.

1. Confess with your mouth the Lord Jesus.

2. And believe in your heart that God has raised Jesus from the dead.

If we take these two steps, there is no need to fear the unpardonable sin.

I Fear the Unknown

It is a normal reaction for people to fear something they don't know about. But you don't have to be in the dark concerning eternal matters. We have His Word—the Holy Bible, and within its pages is everything we need to know about Heaven and eternal life with Jesus, and how to be in right standing with God. It also warns us about hell and our enemy satan, and how to protect ourselves from him and his wickedness, and how to make sure we do not send ourselves there by rejecting Jesus Christ as our Savior.

*Let not your heart be troubled; you believe in God, believe also in Me. In My Father's house are many mansions; if it were not so, I would have told you. I go to prepare a place for you. And if **I go and prepare a place for you**, I will come again and receive you to Myself; that **where I am, there you may be also*** (John 14:1-3).

I Am Afraid of the Possible Pain of Death

Oh, how the enemy loves when we live in fear about things, especially when things have not happened, or may not happen. But this fear is not pleasing to God. The Bible speaks plainly to us about fear and that it does not come from God. It says in Second Timothy 1:7, *"For God has not given us a spirit of fear, but of power and of love and of a sound mind."*

Pray this declaration against the fear of death:

I will not allow the spirit of fear to control me. I take control of my thoughts now. I will not fear death, nor the possible pain of death. I will not live in fear of things that have not happened, or may never happen. I put my trust in my Lord Jesus, and I walk this earth filled with His power, with His love, and with His sound mind. I do possess the mind of Christ in these matters of life and death. I will not focus on the negative things that might happen, but will fix my eyes upon my Redeemer, my Deliverer, and my Reason to Hope instead of lingering in fearful thoughts about death.

PRAY PSALM 91 TO OVERCOME THE FEAR OF DEATH

We are living in perilous and dangerous times, and things in the natural are only going to get worse—but God gives us His promise of divine protection in Psalm 91. Regardless of the hour we live in, His promises remain the same; they never change. This is welcomed good news in this turbulent hour. I believe in the power of praying God's Word over ourselves and our families. Psalm 91 is a power-packed prayer of God's promise of divine protection for us. I encourage you to:

- Read Psalm 91 several times to familiarize yourself with it.
- After you are familiar with it, start with verse 1 and personalize it for yourself.
- Meditate upon His protection.
- Start to memorize this portion of Scripture.
- When fearful thoughts come to taunt you, quote Psalm 91 aloud.
- Allow the power of God's Word to encourage you today.

Let's look at each of the sixteen verses in Psalm 91 verse by verse, staring with verse 1:

1. *"He who dwells in the secret place of the Most High shall abide under the shadow of the Almighty."* It is our responsibility to choose who we spend our time with during these turbulent times. We can spend our time with the spirit of fear, or we can make a quality decision and spend our time with the Lord. There is protection and provision when we are under the boundary of His shadow.

2. *"I will say of the Lord, 'He is my refuge and my fortress; My God, in Him I will trust.'"* Declaring the attributes of the Lord is a powerful, but humble way to address the Lord. He honors our faith in Him. And it also affirms our faith to quote His protection.

3. *"Surely He shall deliver you from the snare of the fowler and from the perilous pestilence."* What encouragement this can stir within us when we vocalize His greatness over our enemy and all of his wicked works.

4. *"He shall cover you with His feathers, and under His wings you shall take refuge; His truth shall be your shield and buckler."* This Scripture verse is visually filled with His tenderness toward us and assures us of His divine protection.

5. *"You shall not be afraid of the terror by night, nor of the arrow that flies by day."* With God we do not need to fear what comes against us in the supernatural realm, nor do we need to be afraid of what could rise against us in the physical realm either. God is with us at all times.

6. *"Nor of the pestilence that walks in darkness, nor of the destruction that lays waste at noonday."* He has given us authority over things that can do us harm.

7. *"A thousand may fall at your side, and ten thousand at your right hand; but it shall not come near you."* Again, we have a boundary of protection as we abide under His shadow.

8. *"Only with your eyes shall you look, and see the reward of the wicked."* It is reassuring to know that we will be spared from the consequences of sin.

9. *"Because you have made the Lord, who is my refuge, even the Most High, your dwelling place."* This is confirmation of our security that we have in Him. And no matter what we face in the days ahead, He is our security.

10. *"No evil shall befall you, nor shall any plague come near your dwelling."* These are great statements of faith to declare over ourselves verbally every day.

11. *"For He shall give His angels charge over you, to keep you in all your ways."* He sends His ministering spirits to protect us from evil.

12. *"In their hands they shall bear you up, lest you dash your foot against a stone."* The angels have been assigned a plan of action on our behalf.

13. *"You shall tread upon the lion and the cobra, the young lion and the serpent you shall trample underfoot."* He gives to us authority over all of our enemies.

14. *"Because he has set his love upon Me, therefore I will deliver him; I will set him on high, because he has known My name."* This is the reason we can activate the power of His redemption.

15. *"He shall call upon Me, and I will answer him; I will be with him in trouble; I will deliver him and honor him."* These words bring assurance to us that no matter what happens in this life, He will respond to our need.

16. *"With long life I will satisfy him, and show him My salvation."* These are promised benefits that come from a personal relationship with God.

These are trying times, and we need to take control over a spirit of fear concerning these last days. Praying the Word of God gives strength and peace to our mind and emotions, and changes our focus from fear to His faithfulness.

DECLARATION OF FAITH TO PRAY FOR PROTECTION

According to the Word of the Lord, I declare what I already possess over myself and my family and friends, in the mighty name of Jesus. And so now, I do declare that I dwell in the shelter of the Most High, and I rest in the shadow of the Almighty. He is my refuge, my fortress, and my God, and I trust Him (Psalm 91:1-2). The Lord is faithful, He will strengthen and protect me from the evil one (2 Thessalonians 3:3). God is my refuge and strength, an ever-present help in trouble (Psalm 46:1). He is my hiding place, and will protect me from trouble and surround me with songs of deliverance (Psalm 32:7).

I sing to God; I sing in praise of His name. I extol Him who rides on the clouds, and I rejoice before Him—His name is the Lord. A Father to the fatherless, a Defender of widows is God in His holy dwelling (Psalm 68:4-5). I cast my cares on the Lord and He sustains me; He will never let the righteous be shaken (Psalm 55:22). I will lie down in peace and sleep, for He alone makes me dwell in safety (Psalm 4:8).

The Lord is my light and my salvation—whom shall I fear? The Lord is the stronghold of my life—of whom shall I be afraid? (Psalm 27:1). I walk securely, because I walk in integrity (Proverbs 10:9). I am prudent; I see danger and take refuge (Proverbs 27:12). He is good, and a refuge in times of trouble. He cares for me because I trust in Him (Nahum 1:7). He keeps me in perfect peace, for my mind is steadfast because I trust in Him (Isaiah 26:3).

The Lord does not take me out of this world but He protects me from the evil one (John 17:15). Because I trust in the Lord and do good, I can dwell in the land and enjoy safe pasture (Psalm 37:3). The name of the Lord is a fortified tower; the righteous run to it and are safe (Proverbs 18:10). He will cover me with His feathers, and under His wings I will find refuge; His faithfulness will be my shield and fortification (Psalm 91:4).

WHAT HAPPENS TO US DURING THE DEATH PROCESS?

One of the biggest fears people face is the fear of death. And one major reason is the fear of the unknown of the death process. What happens to us during this time? Is it as painful as it appears to be?

Many years ago, while I was being heavily attacked by the spirit of death as I have been sharing throughout this work, something happened to me that I am now able to share with you. I have only shared this with a handful of people, but I always knew that one day I would be able to share it publicly, I just had to wait for God's timing. And His timing is now.

I believe what I share will release many Christians from the fear of the death process. It will cause the spirit of death, and its companion, the spirit of fear, to lose power over God's people.

Let me begin my story. I was really struggling with the spirit of death. It was one attack after another in all areas of life. Even when my body was strong and healthy, I would be attacked by death.

I was extremely vulnerable to these attacks right after I ministered to many people during a healing event. As soon as I would step off the platform, every sickness and disease would instantly come upon me.

I remember one such time was when I had just finished an outdoor healing campaign in the Maasai area of Kenya in Africa. I witnessed many healings and creative miracles, deliverances, and salvations. It was a power-packed event. As soon as I stepped off the platform, I started to feel very strange. It was almost as if I had stepped into the supernatural realm, and I believe I had. I looked up at my personal intercessor and travel assistant at that time, and said to her as I fell into her arms, "Pray in the Spirit." I whispered to her, "I'm dying." I kid you not, every sickness and disease that I had just commanded off of people came onto me. I even went instantly deaf in one ear. I collapsed in her arms, and we both prayed in the Spirit until every wicked illness and disease left me in the name of Jesus.

I share this with you to awaken you to the fact that sickness and disease is very spiritual, and the carriers are demons. They look for every opportunity to attack, especially those who are bold enough to take a stand against them. But in the name of Jesus, we do not need to fear these attacks, we just need to be very aware of what's happening around us spiritually, and know how to fight them off of us.

Another time this happened was when I was in Guatemala, tending to my family and all the children in our children's home. There was a period in my life when the attacks of death were unrelenting; I have shared several of these testimonies with you in this work. I don't share them to glorify the spirit of death and its attacks against us, but to teach and train you how to overcome this wicked demon and every one of its attacks against us.

I was under attack and feeling very discouraged by it all. I was sitting outside one night praying to the Lord about what was going on in my life, and I told Him I didn't want to continue with life on this earth if this was how it was going to be. And let me make it perfectly clear to you, I didn't want to die. I just did not want to continue fighting this type of battle. But I had to learn something back then that I have been teaching you throughout this work about the importance of the will to live during heavy battles on earth.

Caught between Two Realms

I no sooner spoke these words out loud to the Lord when all of a sudden I felt very strange. I was immediately leaving the physical realm and entering into the supernatural realm. But during the first moments I was caught between the two realms. I tried to stand up from where I was sitting, but could not; I couldn't even move my legs at first. But I fought through it and got myself up and into the house. My husband looked at me and didn't know what happening to me. And I couldn't tell him, because I couldn't speak at that moment. I was very quickly fading and leaving the earthly realm. I fell into his arms, and he carried me to our bed.

In the natural it looked frightening, but I want to explain to you what I was allowed to learn through all of this. First Corinthians 15:55-57 says, *"'O Death, where is your sting? O Hades, where is your victory?' The sting of death* is *sin, and the strength of sin is the law. But thanks* be *to God, who gives us the victory through our Lord Jesus Christ."*

As I lay in bed, I could not respond to what was going on around me, but I could see through the walls. I could hear everything that was going on. I saw my husband on his knees in our bathroom praying.

My spirit was slowly leaving my physical body. It was lifting up out of me, as if being pulled, even though no one was pulling on it. And I could first feel the death in my body in my feet as my spirit was lifting and no longer inhabiting that area.

And as it was lifting up and out of me, from my shoulders and head area, I was looking down at my physical body. And I can attest that it looked painful. My physical body was working hard through the stage of those last breaths. But as painful as it appeared, there was no pain whatsoever. It was just a departure from the body that housed my spirit all those years.

As soon as my spirit was released from the physical body, I was standing alongside my bed and instantly praising God in a way not possible on earth. There was such freedom—no earthly time or physical limitations, only instant and total joy being with Him in an atmosphere of sheer glory.

Then I was hovering, sitting halfway in the wall above my bed, and Jesus was sitting there with me. My body was still working through laborious breaths of death. But I want to reiterate that there was no pain at all. There is no sorrow or suffering of any kind for the believer in Jesus.

I wasn't looking for loved ones who went on before me. I was with Jesus, I was caught up in His presence, and that's all that mattered. It was so natural to be with Him. It was beautiful in every way.

But all of a sudden I looked at Him and I knew it was not my time to leave earth. I said to Him, "It's not my time to die." I asked Him, "Who is going to call me back into my body?" He answered me ever so gently, "You are." And I did. I said, "In Jesus' name, I call myself back into my body." And the next thing I knew it was about 10 o'clock in the morning.

I want to back up just a bit. While I was still lingering there, and I know now that I was going to be given a choice, I could go and be with Him for eternity, or I could enter back into my body and fulfill my destiny. I had to *choose* to live, fight to win, and conquer this spirit of death.

I remember getting up out of bed and it physically hurt to be inside my body. It was as if my spirit was too big for my physical body and I was clothed in a really tight suit. Then I had to deal with being back on earth, and not with my Lord. But together we worked through it, and I became wiser and stronger from dealing with the spirit of death.

We have faced the fear of death in this chapter. We've taken a real good look at common fears that the enemy tries to use against us in these last days about death. Now, as we move on to our last and final chapter, we are going to find the warrior within us to fight and conquer the spirit of death in these last days.

Prayer

> *Dear Holy Spirit,*
> *I have to admit that I fear death. Forgive me for allowing fear to take over me in these areas. I now know that I have no reason to fear death in these last days, and that Your promises never*

change even though the times do. You are faithful and true to me. Remind me, Holy Spirit, to declare words of faith from Your Holy Word for protection over me and my family during these perilous times. In Jesus' name, I pray, amen.

Pledge

I pledge to God and to myself that I will choose to live, fight to win, and overcome this spirit of death. I will fulfill my destiny on this earth and glorify my Father in Heaven.

Questions for Chapter 14—Facing the Fear of Death in These Last Days

1. How can we overcome overwhelming feelings of fear and insecurity?

2. What are two ways we should pray during these turbulent times?

3. What are four steps to grow your faith?

4. How can we undo regrets with the Lord?

5. What is the unpardonable sin?

6. What two things must we do to be saved?

7. What are the beginning words of John 14:1-3?

Personal Reflection

Am I in a battle with the spirit of death? Am I feeling discouraged and worn down from this battle? Have I made the decision that no matter what I will choose life, fight to win, and conquer the spirit of death?

Group Discussion

Talk about why people fear death. Discuss the reasons mentioned, and perhaps there are other reasons. Look at these reasons through the eyes of the Scriptures. Encourage each other in the faith to choose life, fight to win, and conquer the spirit of death.

Chapter 15

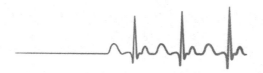

RELEASING THE WARRIOR WITHIN YOU

WORD OF THE LORD

The Spirit of the Lord would say to you this day, "Do not worry, do not fret, and certainly do not forget that My yoke is easy, and My burden is light. I bore your pain and suffering upon My back, so victory while on this earth you would not lack. That old devil will try to bind you with his spirit of fear, but I say, 'Trust Me, for I am ever near.' Do not play the enemy's game, his fame is to laden you with guilt and shame. And his tactics remain the same, and his aim is to lame. While My aim is to release you from his wicked game of shame and blame. I shed My blood to set you free, so you could be all I created you to be—blessed and highly favored. And in this promise I will not waver...

"So set your sights upon My grace, and as you gaze upon My face, know that I am with you to complete your race. Beloved, I love you with a love from up above. Soon the trumpet will blow, and it will be quite the show. My people from all ends of the earth will meet together around the throne, My throne of grace. What a mighty place, filled with a heavenly race,

> *engulfed with the presence of the Almighty. Be dressed and ready, and remain faithful and steady. But while on earth and in eternity to come, victory you will not lack. I've got you covered, I bore it all upon My back."*

Let's look at a few famous biblical warriors—the battles they fought, how God equipped them, and how their heroic stories empower us to victory today.

THE IMPORTANCE OF A CONSECRATED WARRIOR

As warriors for God, we need to learn the importance of being fully consecrated to Him. Let's look to the following warrior examples to learn more. Samson was born to a barren couple after they had been visited by an angel of the Lord foretelling them of his birth. The mother was given instructions about what she could and could not eat or drink, and they were never allowed to cut his hair. These are the words of the Lord concerning their promised son:

> *For behold, you shall conceive and bear a son. And no razor shall come upon his head, for the child shall be a Nazirite to God from the womb; and he shall begin to deliver Israel out of the hand of the Philistines* (Judges 13:5).

When it says that he shall be called a Nazirite, this means he was consecrated or set apart for God's service. This happened while he was still in his mother's womb. The angel of the Lord prophesied how the Lord was going to use him, saying *"and he shall begin to deliver Israel out of the hand of the Philistines."*

Samson was a man of supernatural strength. His secret weapon from God was in his uncut hair. His strength was not actually in his hair, it was a symbol of obedience that began with his parents and he continued in the obedience of what was required of him as being consecrated to God.

But Samson was tempted and fell. He fell into temptation with Delilah who was bribed by his enemy to find out the secret of his strength. Samson gullibly believed Delilah was interested in him, and he toyed with her; but then he lost the game and revealed to her the true secret concerning his strength. Not wasting any time, she cut off his secret weapon and he not only lost his hair, but also God's supernatural strength and His glory over his life. When the Philistines discovered this secret to his strength, they captured him and put out his eyes, making him blind and helpless.

We need to be very aware of the Delilah in our lives. Our enemy will use our gullibility and the people around us to steal our supernatural strength, His manifested glory over us, through the temptation of sin.

But Samson did not need his physical eyes to see his God, his true strength. He repented for his foolish sin and was given another chance. His hair grew back, along with this supernatural strength from God. And one last time, with God's supernatural strength, he pushed and broke down the supporting pillars of the tabernacle and it fell down and destroyed his enemies. (See Judges 13–16.)

When we receive Jesus as Savior, we are to learn to make Him our Lord as well. We are to consecrate ourselves to Him and His service. This doesn't mean we forego haircuts and certain types of food and drink, but that we separate ourselves from the world and its ungodly ways. It is a daily process to surrender all pride in our natural abilities to Him and get to the place of true repentance and dependence upon Him and His supernatural strength. It is in this place of total surrender and dependence on Him that we find our strength to overcome the power, *all* power of the enemy. Jesus gave to us all authority over satan and his wicked works, including premature death and its deadly attacks. (See Luke 10:19.)

As we spend a few moments and reflect on a failure and a success from Samson's life, we see the importance of being fully consecrated to God in our hearts to win our battle.

Let's turn our focus to David and see what the Spirit of the Lord would have us learn from his life that will help us defeat our enemy—the spirit of death, premature death.

SLAY THE GIANT BY GOD'S GRACE

David, who started out as a lowly shepherd boy and eventually was anointed as the king of Israel, is best known for his famous victory against the Philistine warrior—the giant, Goliath.

We will pick up the story of this amazing battle in First Samuel 17 when Goliath challenges the armies of Israel:

> *Then he stood and cried out to the armies of Israel, and said to them, "Why have you come out to line up for battle? Am I not a Philistine, and you the servants of Saul? Choose a man for yourselves, and let him come down to me. If he is able to fight with me and kill me, then we will be your servants. But if I prevail against him and kill him, then you shall be our servants and serve us." And the Philistine said, "I defy the armies of Israel this day; give me a man, that we may fight together." When Saul and all Israel heard these words of the Philistine, they were dismayed and greatly afraid* (1 Samuel 17:8-11).

When Israel's warriors saw Goliath, they ran away in great fear of him. And naturally speaking, they had good reason to do so. He was a giant of a man, fully decked out in the latest weaponry of the time, and he was a skilled warrior. No one stood a chance against this giant.

Perhaps you find yourself like the men of Israel's army at the time, and you are facing a giant in the land that everyone is afraid of. And naturally speaking, there is little to no chance of survival. But I want to encourage you that there is a mighty warrior inside you, waiting to be released.

One such example of this mighty warrior inside us can be found in the life of David. Now, let's pick up in verse 32 of chapter 17, where David is speaking with King Saul:

> *Then David said to Saul, "Let no man's heart fail because of him; your servant will go and fight with this Philistine." And Saul said to David, "You are not able to go against this Philistine to fight with him; for you are a youth, and he a man of war from his youth." But David said to Saul..."Your servant has killed both lion and bear; and this uncircumcised Philistine will be like one of them, seeing he has defied the armies of the living God"* (1 Samuel 17:32-34,36).

Let us take note of a few points in this portion of Scripture. Even though David is just a youth, the youngest of his brothers, and knows he's not much more than a lowly shepherd boy, this doesn't stop him from fighting the giant rising up against them. The truth of the matter is, our age, whether we are young, old, or somewhere in between the two, does not make any difference in matters of faith. Our position and rank in life aren't excuses either to not fight our enemy.

God created us to win, to conquer our enemies no matter how big and powerful they are. And David in his youth proves this to be true.

Saul agrees to allow David to fight Goliath, the giant:

> *So Saul clothed David with his armor, and he put a bronze helmet on his head; he also clothed him with a coat*

of mail. David fastened his sword to his armor and tried to walk, for he had not tested them. And David said to Saul, "I cannot walk with these, for I have not tested them." So David took them off. Then he took his staff in his hand; and he chose for himself five smooth stones from the brook, and put them in a shepherd's bag, in a pouch which he had, and his sling was in his hand. And he drew near to the Philistine (1 Samuel 17:38-40).

Saul offered David the finest suit of armor and weaponry available, but David refused them and removed them. He had not used anything like that before. But he did know how to use his staff and slingshot, so he grabbed five stones. The number five represents grace, and this is what David would need to defeat this fierce giant. He had it, and so do we.

He only used one of the five stones, and hit Goliath in the middle of the forehead. That giant-size warrior fell to the ground, and then David took the sword and cut off his head—and the entire Philistine army fled in fear.

There is a powerful lesson in this true story for us. No matter the size or strength of the giant rising against us, we can utterly defeat it, not with human means, but by the grace of God given to us.

For by grace you have been saved through faith, and that not of yourselves; it is the gift of God, not of works, lest anyone should boast (Ephesians 2:8-9).

THE CARE OF THE GOOD SHEPHERD

As a shepherd, David learned great truths about God that would carry him through many battles in life. He saw God as his Shepherd, and himself as one of His sheep—as we all are. He knew firsthand that sheep are dependent upon the care of the shepherd, and a good shepherd tends well to his sheep. David had such a deep working knowledge of this spiritual concept that he wrote about it in Psalm 23. We so often hear this psalm recited at funerals, but is it really about death? Or did David have another purpose all together when he wrote it? Let's find out what this psalm is about.

David wrote, *"The Lord is my shepherd; I shall not want"* (Psalm 23:1). He knew that God was the good Shepherd. And Jesus also calls Himself the Good Shepherd in John 10:11, *"I am the good shepherd. The good shepherd gives His life for the sheep."* And with Him overseeing David's life, he would have no lack. His needs would be met. This is actually quite amazing faith considering he was a shepherd boy. It was not a glamorous position, nor was it a high-paying one. But he was assured in the faithfulness of the Good Shepherd toward His sheep that he would be taken care of.

And not just taken care of, but well provided for too. David goes on to write, *"He makes me to lie down in green pastures; He leads me beside the still waters"* (Psalm 23:2). Not only would God provide pastures to graze upon, but they would be green and fertile pastures with plenty of food and other comforts necessary to sustain life, such as water. Not just any water, but *still waters.* Sheep are not swimmers and they would drown in turbulent waters, so David uses this example of the loving Shepherd and how He leads us to safety, not into harm's way.

As David continues to write, he says, *"He restores my soul; He leads me in the paths of righteousness for His name's sake"* (Psalm 23:3). There are many pathways; and like sheep, we can easily be led astray down the wrong ones. But He leads us back onto the path of righteousness. His ways are not only godly, but they lead us to peaceful living. And His righteous lifestyle refreshes our mind and emotions.

"Yea, though I walk through the valley of the shadow of death, I will fear no evil; for You are with me; Your rod and Your staff, they comfort me" (Psalm 23:4) As with any trade, the shepherd has special weapons and

tools. In this portion of Scripture, David mentions a rod. A rod is a stick to use as a weapon for protection. Our Good Shepherd—Jesus—has many ways of protecting us from death, but the weapon behind these ways is His redemptive blood. And even though He shed His blood for us so many years ago, it has never lost its power, and it never will.

David also talks about a staff. A shepherd's staff is a long, sturdy stick with a hook at one end used to manage the sheep, and sometimes used to catch one that's going astray. It can also be used as a weapon to ward off predators. It can also be used as support and to help balance the shepherd on rocky terrain.

When I compare the physical use of an earthly shepherd's staff to our Savior's staff, I can't help but see His Word being the spiritual staff He uses to bring balance back into our lives, to hook us back onto the straight and narrow path when we are getting out of line in our spiritual walk. And we can lean upon His staff for support when we are walking on the rough terrains of life, such as the valley of the shadow of death.

And allow me to make another point concerning this valley of the shadow of death. If and when you find yourself in this valley, you have a choice to make. You can either keep walking through it to the fulfillment of death, or you can stop, turn around, and walk back out of it. The decision belongs to you. According to the next portion of this well-known psalm, God has also provided you with everything you need to conquer and win this battle.

"You prepare a table before me in the presence of my enemies; You anoint my head with oil; My cup runs over..." (Psalm 23:5). Up until now, I believe Psalm 23 was being written in the memory of David as the shepherd boy, but now it is being written from the mindset of King David. And in either position he, like us, has enemies. But in the midst of these attacks from our enemies, the Good Shepherd prepares a bountiful table before us with everything we need to fight and win our

battles, from weapons and tools, to our daily needs being met, and met well, along with guidance and protection.

"You anoint my head with oil...." This anointing is like a refreshing for celebration. Imagine you were the enemy and the ones you were attacking stopped, sat down at a banquet table, and started to refresh themselves to celebrate. I would think this would send a clear message, like no other, filled with confidence of victory, like the battle is already won. I believe that would make the enemy feel flustered and confused. It would be a bit unnerving to say the least. Wouldn't you agree? He continues to write, *"...My cup runs over."* This is referring to abundance. The cup isn't just comfortably full, it is abundantly full, so much so that it is spilling all over, enough to share with others.

David completes this psalm with the following thoughts, *"Surely goodness and mercy shall follow me all the days of my life; and I will dwell in the house of the Lord forever"* (Psalm 23:6). What a beautiful declaration of faith this is. He is declaring without a doubt, no matter where he is, God's goodness and mercy will with him and he will abide with the Lord all the days of his life.

So you see this psalm is not really about death, but about a loving Shepherd who tends well to His sheep and sees to it that their needs are met—met abundantly and affectionately, and protected from the dangers of the enemy.

THE IMPORTANCE OF
OBEDIENCE AND FAITH

As we have studied the biblical warriors Samson and David, we are gleaning spiritual truths that equip us for our seemingly impossible battles as well. But there are a few more points I want to bring to your attention that will help you overcome the spirit of death. Let's turn our attention and consider Joshua and how he and the Israelites marched around the walls of Jericho, and how those fortified walls came tumbling down, not by physical might, but by the power of the Lord.

The Lord sent an angel to Joshua to deliver God's plan of action.

> *Then the Lord said to Joshua, "See, I have delivered Jericho into your hands, along with its king and its fighting men. March around the city once with all the armed men. Do this for six days. Have seven priests carry trumpets of rams' horns in front of the ark. On the seventh day, march around the city seven times, with the priests blowing the trumpets. When you hear them sound a long blast on the trumpets, have the whole army give a loud shout; then the wall of the city will collapse and the army will go up, everyone straight in"* (Joshua 6:2-5 NIV).

This is sort of an unusual battle plan, but it does catch the eye of the unbeliever when successfully implemented. Humans surely cannot take credit for it.

> *On the seventh day, they got up at daybreak and marched around the city seven times in the same manner, except that on that day they circled the city seven times. The seventh time around, when the priests sounded the trumpet blast, Joshua commanded the army, "Shout! For the Lord has given you the city!" When the trumpets sounded, the army shouted, and at the sound of the trumpet, when the men gave a loud shout, the wall collapsed; so everyone charged straight in, and they took the city* (Joshua 6:15-16,20).

Joshua obediently carried out God's plan with His supernatural way to victory using the Ark of the Covenant, marching people, seven priests blowing ram horns, and people shouting together in harmony according the word of the Lord.

Sometimes God's plan for His people doesn't make sense to our human reasoning, but that's the point I am trying to stress here. To overcome our enemy—and in this work we are zeroing in on how to overcome our enemy, the spirit of premature death—our weaponry is not carnal. God's supernatural weapons He commands us to use are faith and obedience to His words of promised victory.

What was Joshua's strength? According to Deuteronomy 34:9 (NIV), it was that he was full of the spirit of wisdom: *"Now Joshua son of Nun was filled with the spirit of wisdom because Moses had laid his hands on him. So the Israelites listened to him and did what the Lord had commanded Moses."*

God gives to us His wisdom as well—the Word of God. We are taught what happens when we do what Joshua was commanded to do: *"Keep this Book of the Law always on your lips; meditate on it day and night, so that you may be careful to do everything written in it. Then you will be prosperous and successful"* (Joshua 1:8 NIV).

This word "meditate" is from the Hebrew word *hagah* and means to ponder upon it and to speak it out (Strong's H1897). And not only are we to ponder upon the Word of God and speak it aloud, but we are to live it. And when we do, we are promised that we will be prosperous and successful, not only in life, but in the daily battles that we face.

Perhaps you feel a bit frightened by these battles. I believe Joshua did too as in the first chapter of Joshua he is told to be *strong and courageous* four times. (See Joshua 1:6-7,9,18.) But despite insecurities, he fought and won the battle at Jericho by obedience and faith in God's plan of action. In Joshua 6:27, there's another secret to Joshua's success, *"So the Lord was with Joshua, and his fame spread throughout all the country."* God was with Joshua, and He is with you. Allow Jesus to be famous through your life.

But indeed for this purpose I have raised you up, that I may show My power in you, and that My name may be declared in all the earth (Exodus 9:16).

An overview of the strengths learned from these warriors:

1. Consecrate our hearts to God.

2. Be aware of the enemy's tactics to steal our supernatural strength and God's glory.

3. The battle is won in God's strength, not our strength.

4. We have His grace to conquer our enemy.

5. We are to depend upon the care of the Good Shepherd.

6. We are to activate faith and obedience to His promises.

7. Activate the power of the spoken word.

8. We are to be bold and courageous.

EQUIPPED WITH SUFFICIENT COURAGE

We are warriors for God and have been equipped in every way necessary to conquer satan and the spirit of death. He has given us sufficient courage that Jesus will be exalted in our bodies. We find an uplifting promise about this sufficient courage in Philippians 1:20 (NIV): *"I eagerly expect and hope that I will in no way be ashamed, but will have sufficient courage so that now as always Christ will be exalted in my body, whether by life or by death."* We do not need to be fearful warriors, but courageous ones.

As God's warrior, utilize this sufficient courage and make it work for you. When the enemy taunts you with death, declare the life of God within you, defy his death report, and dare to live. When he frightens you with thoughts of defeat, shout the victory, and remind him of what he's got coming to him. The truth of the matter in all of this is the enemy would not bother with you and your miraculous victory if he wasn't afraid of what is about to happen in your life for the glory of the Lord. So he is trying to set you on a detour with his fear tactics.

A WOMAN OF FAITH AND COURAGE

I would like to share about a woman in the Bible who modeled sufficient courage in the midst of an attack by the spirit of death.

Esther was Jewish girl, orphaned and then adopted by her cousin, Mordecai. She was taken to the king of the Persian Empire and became part of his harem. She became the queen, but King Xerxes did not know of her Jewish heritage. This was kept a secret from him.

The king had an advisor named Haman who hated Mordecai because he would not bow to him. So in his hatred for Haman, he designed a plan to kill the Jewish people.

Haman said to King Ahasuerus:

> *There is a certain people scattered and dispersed among the people in all the provinces of your kingdom; their laws are different from all other people's, and they do not keep the king's laws. Therefore it is not fitting for the king to let them remain. If it pleases the king, let a decree be written that they be destroyed, and I will pay ten thousand talents of silver into the hands of those who do the work, to bring it into the king's treasuries* (Esther 3:8-9).

As queen, what could she do to save her people? Her cousin Mordecai urged her to speak to the king about the plight of her people and encouraged her with these words:

> *For if you remain completely silent at this time, relief and deliverance will arise for the Jews from another place, but you and your father's house will perish. Yet who knows*

*whether you have come to the kingdom for such a time as
this?* (Esther 4:14)

At great risk she did as Mordecai had requested, and the result of
her example of sufficient courage was that her people were saved from
Haman's wicked plot of mass genocide.

Is God speaking to your heart to speak up and overcome a wicked
plot of satan? Are you to stand up against the spirit of death and fight
the battle for your loved ones? As a warrior for God you can do this.
He has given you everything you need to conquer and win too. Like
Mordecai said to Esther, *"Yet who knows whether you have come to the
kingdom for such a time as this?"* I believe we already know that now is
the time, and the time is short. God is calling His people to take a stand
and rise up in these last days and conquer the spirit of death attacking
our loved ones.

THE KEYS OF DEATH AND HADES

As a warrior for our King Jesus, we need to take our orders from Him.
And as mentioned earlier in this work, we are commissioned to go out
into all the world, not in our own strength, but in the power of His
strength and share the message of eternal life to the lost and dying of
this world.

Jesus has made the way for us to do this successfully. He says in
Revelation 1:18, *"I am He who lives, and was dead, and behold, I am
alive forevermore. Amen. And I have the keys of Hades and of Death."*

There are spiritual keys that unlock certain doors, and since the
death and resurrection of Jesus, the keys of death and hades are now
owned by Him. Because He has the master key to death and hades, He
can now release anyone who believes and confesses that He is Lord from
the eternal fate of death and hell. This supernatural key is authority
over satan and gives to Jesus all authority over all of his wicked works.

246

But God needs His warriors to do His bidding for Him.

> *Whoever calls on the name of the Lord shall be saved. How then shall they call on Him in whom they have not believed? And how shall they believe in Him of whom they have not heard? And how shall they hear without a preacher? And how shall they preach unless they are sent? As it is written: "How beautiful are the feet of those who preach the gospel of peace, who bring glad tidings of good things!"* (Romans 10:13-15)

THREE IMPORTANT THINGS JESUS DID FOR US

As warriors for God, let us not lose sight of what Jesus actually did for us. As we've seen throughout this work, Jesus suffered and died at Calvary, and rose from the dead in our place so that we could be released from what we really deserve, eternal suffering in hell. First Peter 3:18 tells us, *"For Christ also suffered once for sins, the just for the unjust, that He might bring us to God, being put to death in the flesh but made alive by the Spirit."*

Galatians 3:13 says, *"Christ has redeemed us from the curse of the law, having become a curse for us (for it is written, 'Cursed is everyone who hangs on a tree')."* Jesus redeemed us from the curse by becoming the curse for us. This word "redeem" comes from the Greek word *exagorazō* and means by payment of a price to recover from the power of another, to ransom, or to buy off (Strong's G1805). Jesus paid the price once and for all with the payment of His innocent blood to deliver us from the consequences of our willful sin—the curse. And because of this great and eternal gift, we can activate every promise of His, if we will believe.

Another amazing thing He did for us by His suffering and death at Calvary is that He restored fellowship between God and people.

Romans 5:10 talks about this reconciliation, *"For if when we were ene-mies we were reconciled to God through the death of His Son, much more, having been reconciled, we shall be saved by His life."*

Review of the three things He did for us:

1. He suffered and died in our place at Calvary, and rose from the dead for us.

2. He redeemed us from the curse by becoming the curse for us.

3. He reconciled people back to God, restoring the fellowship between us with the power of His blood.

RESURRECTION POWER

After taking back the keys of death and hades, He rose from the dead. And in doing so He emboldened us with that same Spirit that raised Christ from the dead, and His Holy Spirit now dwells in us: *"But if the Spirit of Him who raised Jesus from the dead dwells in you, He who raised Christ from the dead will also give life to your mortal bodies through His Spirit who dwells in you"* (Romans 8:11).

This is an amazing faith gift we have been given—resurrection power in Him. We have the authority backed by the redemptive blood of Jesus to raise the dead, and to even resurrect dead body parts.

And as you have read through some wonderful healing testimonies, this is happening all around the world, and probably in your own neighborhood too. The Spirit of God is moving—take the limits off of Him.

COMING INTO ONE ACCORD WITH THE SPIRIT OF LIFE

To overcome the spirit of death, we must come into one accord with the Spirit of Life—the Holy Spirit. We must align ourselves with the Word of God that declares by the whips Jesus endured for us at the whipping post that we are healed.

> But [in fact] He has borne our griefs, and He has carried our sorrows and pains; yet we [ignorantly] assumed that He was stricken, struck down by God and degraded and humiliated [by Him]. But He was wounded for our transgressions, He was crushed for our wickedness [our sin, our injustice, our wrongdoing]; the punishment [required] for our well-being fell on Him, and **by His stripes (wounds) we are healed** (Isaiah 53:4-5 AMP).

He has already paid the price for all to be healed—saved and unsaved. Now again, He is waiting on us, His warriors, to get out there where the sick people are and release His healing power to all those around us. And if you, the warrior is sick and suffering, train yourself in the Bible and believe and receive all that He has provided for you, including your healing.

CURSE THE SPIRIT OF DEATH

As God's warriors, we need to learn how to speak His healing language. With the power of the Holy Spirit we curse with our words to invoke death and harm to the spirit of death and the sickness or disease inflicting harm to our body. We have the spiritual right to do this because Jesus became the curse for us to redeem us from it when He hung upon the Cross.

How would we go about verbalizing a curse against death? If the curse of death is cancer, with all authority given to you by Jesus say, *"I curse the spirit of death and this cancer and all its cells and tumors at their very seeds, and command them to dry up at their roots and be eliminated from this body, in Jesus' name."* If the curse of death is diabetes, say with the same authority, "In the name of Jesus, I curse this spirit of death and the power of diabetes, and the high levels of blood glucose in my body." Whatever disease that the spirit of death is inflicting upon you or your loved ones—curse it in the name of Jesus.

RELEASE THE SPIRIT OF LIFE

After cursing the spirit of death, we release the Spirit of Life within us. We permit the Spirit of Life freedom to reign in our physical bodies.

> *I release the Spirit of Life, the Holy Spirit, to flow in and throughout my (or name of another) being, resurrect what is dead, awaken what is dormant, recreate what is destroyed. I speak to every cell, tissue, organ and system in this body to align itself with the Word of God that declares by His stripes I (or name of loved one) is healed and made whole, spiritually, emotionally, mentally, and physically, all for the glory of Jesus.*

Speak Life

Remember, speak life, healing, and creative miracles. Speak to your loved one and give him or her a reason to turn around in the valley of the shadow of death, and return to this earth to fulfill their calling and destiny in the name of Jesus.

Live Life

I tell you, it is not enough to just speak life, but we have to then activate our faith and live life with the mindset that we will fulfill our destiny, glorifying our God the entire way on this journey called life.

As a warrior for God, you lack nothing necessary for success. You have been given all that you need to conquer the spirit of death and live victoriously for yourself and for those you love. Now God is waiting on you—release the warrior within you for His glory.

Declaration of Faith to Pray

I will pick up the strength of the shield of faith and activate the Sword of the Spirit. By the power of the Word of God I will decree and cut off with my words the evil power of the enemy that tries to entangle me. I align the power of my words with my Lord, and declare that *"Yes, I am more than a conqueror."*

With the mind of Christ, I will remember to whom I belong and who He says I am. I am His and He is mine. I am the bride of Christ, and I will cherish the relationship I have with my groom—Jesus. I will tend well to that childlike faith and boldly defeat my enemies—satan and the spirit of death.

I have been enlightened by the Word of God, and this heavy weight of the enemy I will no longer bear. I cast off all worry, and I return it to where it rightfully belongs, at the feet of Jesus, where I humbly surrender all doubt and unbelief. I trust in the power of His might instead—not in the strength of disease and death.

I love God because He first loved me. All that I ever need I find in the midst of His great love for me. I can never earn His love, and I can never lose His love. He loves me because He does, and that settles the matter.

I am created to win, and to live life on earth in His victory. With this revelation knowledge I will encourage, pray, and activate my faith for others, as well as for myself.

I will not fear sudden and unexpected battles—I will rest knowing that my God will make a way when there is no way in the natural. I have total victory over all deadly attacks.

I plead the power of the blood of Jesus over myself and my loved ones. I declare that no weapon formed against us shall prosper. No evil will come near my dwelling. I overcome by His blood that He willingly shed for me.

Jesus is my Good Shepherd, I know His voice, and to another I will not listen. He leads me into His green pastures of victory and gives to me the drink of life—His living waters. With the protection of His rod and the strength of His staff, I will fear no evil.

I am equipped with sufficient courage, and God will be exalted in my body for the glory of God, amen.

Pledge to Overcome the Spirit of Death

I pledge to God and to myself to become the mighty warrior God intended me to be. I consecrate my heart to Him. I will keep a watchful eye against the Delilah that would try to come and cause me to spiritually fall and cause me to lose my supernatural strength from the glory of God. I will depend upon His grace to defeat the attacks of the giants that rise up against me, and I will glorify God with my physical being. I will not die prematurely. I will live and fulfill my calling and destiny for the glory of the Lord Jesus Christ.

Questions for Chapter 15—Releasing the Warrior within You

1. Samson's uncut hair was a symbol of what?

2. How will the enemy use the Delilah in our life to attack us?

3. How do we consecrate ourselves to God?

4. What is inside us?

5. What is the mighty warrior waiting for?

6. What does the number 5 represent?

7. What did David need to fight the giant?

8. No matter the size or strength of the giant rising against us, we can utterly defeat it, not with human means but how?

9. How did David see God and himself?

10. What does Jesus call Himself in John 10:11?

11. With the Good Shepherd overseeing David's life what would he not have?

12. What type of pastures will He lead us to?

13. Why does the shepherd lead the sheep to still waters?

14. What does His righteous lifestyle refresh?

15. What is the shepherd's rod and what is it used for?

16. Our Good Shepherd—Jesus—has many ways of protecting us from death, but what is the weapon behind these ways?

17. In the midst of the attacks from our enemies, what does the Good Shepherd prepare for us?

18. What are some of the items mentioned on this table?

19. What is David declaring when he says, *"Surely goodness and mercy shall follow me all the days of my life; and I will dwell in the house of the Lord forever"*?

20. Joshua obediently carried out God's plan with His supernatural ways to victory using what?

21. What supernatural weapons does God command us to use to win our battles?

22. What were Mordecai's famous words to Queen Esther about time?

23. Who does God need to do His bidding for Him?

24. From our reading what are three things Jesus did for us?

25. To overcome the spirit of death, what must we do with the Spirit of Life?

26. With the power of the Holy Spirit, what do we do with our words to the spirit of death?

27. After cursing the spirit of death, what do we do with the Spirit of Life?

28. According to our reading, what do we do with life?

29. Speaking words of life alone is not enough, what else do we need to do?

Personal Reflection

As I take a few moments to reflect on being a warrior for God, I ask myself the hard questions:

- Have I truly consecrated my heart to Him?

- Am I aware of any attacks of the enemy to steal my supernatural strength and God's glory from my life?

- Am I dependent upon His strength to win this battle? Or do I continue to try to win in my own human strength?

- Am I activating His grace to conquer this enemy in my life?

- Am I dependent upon the care of the Good Shepherd? Or am I trying to take care of this situation on my own?

- Have I honestly, without a shadow of a doubt, activated faith and obedience to His promise to me in this circumstance?

- Am I speaking right words?

- Am I bold and courageous? Or am I struggling with fear in this matter?

Group Discussion

Ask for the cooperation of the group to share honestly from their hearts about being a warrior for God. Have we all consecrated our hearts to God? If not, would anyone like to do this now? Have them repeat a prayer to God about consecrating their hearts and their ways to Him. Talk about trying to defeat the enemy in their own strength versus in the strength of the Holy Spirit. Have we honestly activated faith and obedience to the promises of God? If not, should we pray a prayer of repentance in the matter? Am I speaking God's promises or my feelings over myself and the present situation? As warriors for Jesus, are we being bold and courageous? Or are we struggling with fear over the matter?

Appendix

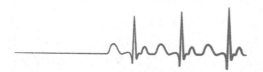

ANSWERS FOR CHAPTER-END QUESTIONS

ANSWERS FOR CHAPTER 1— THE SPIRIT OF DEATH

1. The word "renounce" means to cast off or reject, as a connection or possession; to forsake; as, to renounce the world and all its cares.

2. If you don't know who your enemy is, you will engage in combat with your fellow soldiers, your allies—those who are sent to help.

3. The word "ally" comes from the Latin word *alligare*, meaning to bind to, like nations who are allies in wartime will act together and protect one another.

4. The spirit of death is a powerful demon that is bent upon your destruction to provoke premature death in your physical body.

5. Satan's strategies against us.

6. Deadly operations against us include weapons of mass destruction such as sickness, rare and incurable disease, deterioration of any

type against the physical body, lying spirits that induce thoughts of suicide and murder, including abortion.

ANSWERS FOR CHAPTER 2— NEGATIVE EMOTIONS PARTNER WITH THE SPIRIT OF DEATH

1. Death.

2. A spirit of fear.

3. The devil wants to isolate you so you become more vulnerable to his wicked attacks.

4. Death.

5. Still your heart before Him. Worship Him in spirit and in truth. Pray in the Spirit. Fellowship with Him in His Word. Stop doing all the talking, and just be quiet and let Him speak to your heart.

6. When it lingers.

7. Depression lingers when we live in the emotional realm of past hurts and disappointments.

8. Because we focus on the problem, and in doing so we wind up magnifying our enemy, the devil.

9. Lies.

ANSWERS FOR CHAPTER 3—UNDERSTANDING SPIRITUAL FORCES AND ACTIVITIES

1. God.

2. The Giver of Life.

3. Eternal life and abundant life on earth.

4. Everything He does creates and supports life—now and forever.

5.   Satan.

6.   Lucifer.

7.   He became prideful about his beauty.

8.   He was evicted from Heaven and cast away from the holy presence of God.

9.   Angels are ministering spirits sent to serve those who will inherit salvation.

10. These ministering spirits are sent by God to deliver divine messages, reveal God's plans and truths, warn of imminent dangers, help us escape disasters, help us fight battles, frustrate the enemy's plans, open and close doors, and help us in many other ways.

11. The angel rebuked him and said, "Don't do that!"

12. From this portion of Scripture, we can conclude that any angel that allows us to bow down and worship it is not of God, but a demon in disguise.

13. Demons are fallen angels.

14. Satan is the leader of demons.

15. They carry out the works of satan to steal, to kill, and to destroy us.

ANSWERS FOR CHAPTER 4—CREATED TO WIN

1.   A battle plan.

2.   A reason to fight.

3.   A goal or goals to achieve.

4.   A reason to believe you can win the battle.

5.   A blood covenant.

6.   It cannot be broken.

7.   Stand.

8. The power of His might.

9. It protects us from the deceptive lies of the enemy. It keeps us honorable and upright in all of God's ways. God's truth also covers us with integrity, preventing us from being exposed to the world's sinful ways.

10. The redemptive work of Christ.

11. The Word of God.

12. The shield of faith.

13. To save, to heal, and to make whole.

14. We are.

15. God wills that we take responsibility, grow up in the faith, activate it and part the Red Sea that is preventing us from entering the Promised Land.

ANSWERS FOR CHAPTER 5—ENCOURAGE, PRAY, AND ACTIVATE FAITH

1. First, because most are not being trained in the faith from the pulpit; second, you hold back because you're not sure what to say.

2. Spend time with the hurting, be sincere, and listen to them.

3. Pray and ask the Holy Spirit to lead you and guide you.

4. The Lord might use them to catapult these people into the realm of the supernatural power of the Holy Spirit where the answer to their needs manifest.

5. Be sincere, listen as if you truly care, don't be preachy or condescending, share words of hope and offer to pray in faith with them.

6. A request or petition for ourselves.

7. A prayer on the behalf of others.

8. Our prayers of faith will save the sick, forgive sins, they will heal one another, and our effective, fervent prayers will avail, profit much.

9. It is bound to the command of our words.

10. They will recover.

11. Believe.

12. No.

13. Reading and studying the Bible about it.

14. They need to possess the will to live.

ANSWERS FOR CHAPTER 6—SUDDEN AND UNEXPECTED BATTLES

1. Because we were a threat to the enemy and the darkness he planned against other people.

2. Go deeper in prayer for the protection of my family.

3. A decree of faith.

4. One time doesn't cover all time.

5. Declare what you already have in your spiritual possession.

6. As a believer of the Almighty God, you are a threat to satan and his demonic force.

7. Your time on this earth to be a mighty witness for Christ.

8. Call out to God in faith right now.

9. It should be from your heart, sincere and full of faith that He is the One to help you in your time of need.

10. To hear you speak to Him in His language—faith.

11. Boldly before His throne of grace.

12. Your faith.

13. It becomes stronger and more powerful.

ANSWERS FOR CHAPTER 7—GOD MAKES A WAY

1. We put our trust in our God who is far superior than the danger we face.

2. Yes.

3. The experiences are a result of something much deeper than amazing testimonies.

4. His faithfulness to each of us.

5. He remains faithful.

6. His faithfulness will make a way of escape to protect us from the wicked plans of satan.

7. Enter into true fellowship with Him.

8. To restore the personal fellowship between God and people.

9. I could not think about death, only about living.

10. Many more would have the complete victory they seek.

11. It means to catch (away, up), pluck, pull, take (by force).

12. The Holy Spirit plucked or pulled (translated) Philip from one place to another place on this earth supernaturally.

13. By faith.

14. The Greek word *euaresteō* which means to gratify entirely.

15. It means to be translated, carry over, remove, change or turn.

16. He was taken away, translated, removed from this earth so that he would not see death.

17. It means to go up, ascend, to climb.

18. A great chariot of fire descended and separated Elijah from his disciple, Elisha, and Elijah ascended in a whirlwind into the sky until he saw him no more.

19. The Greek word *epairō*, which means to lift up, raise up, raise on high.

20. One day all of us who believe in the Lord Jesus Christ will hear that great trumpet blow, and we will be instantly translated, caught up, plucked up from this earth to meet Him face to face in the clouds.

ANSWERS FOR CHAPTER 8—VICTORY OVER DEADLY ATTACKS

1. Perilous times.

2. Violent people.

3. Preserve our life.

4. To trust God and to pray.

5. He called out to God with sincerity of heart, *"Help me!"*

6. He saves us from our enemies.

7. Warring angels were dispatched to rescue him.

8. They bought the Israelites time to reach the safety of the other side.

9. We create a shield of protection around us that is very difficult for the enemy to break through.

10. Spend more time in prayer interceding for the protection of our families.

ANSWERS FOR CHAPTER 9—
THE SPIRIT OF SUICIDE

1. Speak up and tell the truth.

2. In the name of Jesus.

3. We take away their demonic artillery against our loved ones.

4. Hope.

5. With sincerity of heart and with words of encouragement.

6. Yes.

7. Fast for them for three days, and pray for them between the hours of 2:00-4:00 A.M.

8. "I love you, and I'm glad you are alive."

ANSWERS FOR CHAPTER 10—
ALCOHOL AND DRUG ADDICTION

1. No, it's a sin.

2. It's an evil spirit, a demon that has taken control of the mind and the emotions and works its evil into the physical realm of the individual and all those they come in contact with.

3. That you have a problem, and it's a sin issue.

4. Do whatever is necessary to be free from this ungodly behavior.

5. No.

6. Because the redemptive power of the blood of Jesus is greater than addiction.

7. Healed, delivered, and made whole in the name of Jesus.

8. If you don't forgive them, your sins will not be forgiven.

9. If you forgive them, your sins are forgiven.

ANSWERS FOR CHAPTER 11— FOLLOWING THE VOICE OF HOPE

1. To be filled with sickness and disease, and to desire to stop living, or to end the life of another.

2. Spirit beings filled with the breath of God housed in human bodies while on this earth.

3. It begins with love—His great love for us.

4. He still loves us as if we are at our best.

5. They see through a tainted glass of impurity.

6. Through His eyes—the clarity of love.

7. It is the power of true hope and faith.

8. God is *and* willing to do exceedingly abundantly above all that we ask or think.

9. *"Let us therefore come boldly unto the throne of grace, that we may obtain mercy, and find grace to help in time of need."*

10. They can easily fall into a pit of despair and become desperate and easily swayed by lying spirits.

11. Discern a lying spirit of hopelessness and be able to distinguish who is speaking to us.

12. No.

13. The voice of God.

14. No, He will not.

15. That we are unfaithful to believe what He says is true.

16. A voice of hope that leads people to the heavenly Father who loves us and is good.

17. We can overflow with confidence in His promises to us.

ANSWERS FOR CHAPTER 12—OVERCOMING BY THE BLOOD OF THE LAMB

1. Atonement is the reconciliation between God and people by the sacrificial offering of Jesus' blood at Calvary.

2. *Hagiazō* and it means to make holy, purify, or to consecrate.

3. The blood of Jesus purifies us and makes us holy onto Him. His blood consecrates us, it separates us from our sinful nature and sets us apart for Him.

4. "Justified" comes from a Greek word *dikaioō*, which means to render just or innocent—free.

5. Grace means goodwill, lovingkindness, and favor.

6. *Apolytrōsis*, which means a releasing effected by payment of ransom.

7. Forgiveness of sins, redemption, deliverance, eternal life, abundant life, supernatural healing, and divine protection.

8. Death and damnation.

9. Be about our heavenly Father's business and return to the true gospel message of the redemptive blood of Jesus Christ and preach and minister with His authority with signs and wonders following and the captives set free.

10. Confess with your mouth the Lord Jesus and believe in your heart that God has raised Him from the dead.

11. Deliverance from a spirit of death; a recreated body part; an inner healing of the soul.

12. According to His riches in glory by Christ Jesus.

13. A lack of knowledge.

14. *"No weapon formed against me and my family will prosper, in Jesus' name."*

ANSWERS FOR CHAPTER 13— DECLARING AND PRAISING YOUR WAY OUT OF PREMATURE DEATH

1. The power of life and death.

2. He uses his words with restraint, calmness, and self-control.

3. Their souls are kept from troubles.

4. Deep waters.

5. We on this earth.

6. We are to call those things that do not exist as if they did.

7. Prophesy either life or death.

8. To live and fulfill our destiny on earth.

9. Their future.

10. *Thelō,* which means to will, to have in mind, to intend, to be resolved, to be determined, to purpose, to desire, to wish, to love, or to like to do a thing.

11. *Dynamai,* which means able, powerful and strong.

12. *Katharizō,* which means to cleanse, to purge, and to purify.

13. Take the situation to the Lord.

14. People of like faith.

15. Curse it.

16. The healing power of the Holy Spirit.

17. Creative miracles to take place.

18. That His healing power is activated in your body.

19. Self-pity.

20. Be persistent and don't stop.

ANSWERS FOR CHAPTER 14—FACING THE FEAR OF DEATH IN THESE LAST DAYS

1. Pray.

2. Pray in tongues, and pray prayers that include Scriptures from the Word of God.

3. Daily read the Bible, talk about its message with Him and with others, speak His promises out loud, and do what the Word tells us to do.

4. By asking His forgiveness for them.

5. Denying Jesus Christ as Lord and Savior.

6. Confess with your mouth the Lord Jesus, and believe in your heart that God has raised Him from the dead.

7. *"Let not your heart be troubled."*

ANSWERS FOR CHAPTER 15—RELEASING THE WARRIOR WITHIN YOU

1. Obedience to being consecrated to God.

2. He will use our gullibility and the people around us to steal our supernatural strength, God's manifested glory over us, through the temptation of sin.

3. We separate ourselves from the world and its ungodly ways.

4. A mighty warrior.

5. To be released.

6. Grace.

7. God's grace.

8. By the grace of God given to us.

9. God as his Shepherd, and himself as one of His sheep.

10. The Good Shepherd.

11. Lack.

12. Green and fertile pastures with plenty of food and other comforts necessary to sustain life.

13. Sheep are not swimmers and they would drown in turbulent waters, so David uses this example of the loving Shepherd and how He leads us to safety—not into harm's way.

14. Our mind and emotions.

15. A stick to use as a weapon for protection.

16. His redemptive blood.

17. A bountiful table before us with everything we need to fight and win our battles.

18. From weapons and tools to our daily needs being met, and met well, along with guidance and protection.

19. He is declaring without a doubt, no matter where he is, God's goodness and mercy will be there. And he will abide, stay with the Lord, all the days of his life.

20. The Ark of the Covenant, marching people, seven priests blowing ram horns, and people shouting together in harmony according the word of the Lord.

21. He commands us to use our faith and obedience to His words of promised victory.

22. *"Yet who knows whether you have come to the kingdom for such a time as this?"*

23. His warriors.

24. He suffered and died in our place at Calvary and rose from the dead for us; He redeemed us from the curse by becoming the curse for us; and He reconciled people back to God, restoring the fellowship between us with the power of His blood.

25. Come into one accord.

26. We curse with our words, death to the spirit of death and the sickness or disease inflicting harm to our body.

27. We release the Spirit of Life within us.

28. We speak it.

29. We have to activate our faith and live life.

About the Author

Becky Dvorak is the author of *DARE to Believe, Greater Than Magic, The Healing Creed, The Prophetic and Healing Power of Your Words,* and is a content partner with Spirit Led Woman / Charisma. She is a prophetess and healing evangelist who conducts healing services, seminars, and conferences globally. After being full-time missionaries since 1994 with her husband, David, in Guatemala, Central America, Becky now resides in the United States. Becky and David are the founders of Healing and Miracles International, Vida Ilimitada, and Life Tender Mercy Children's Home. They are celebrating thirty-nine years of marriage and have eight children—three adult biological, five adopted—one son-in-law, five daughters-in-law, and ten grandchildren.